Ludwig Binswanger and Fernand Deligny
on the Human Condition

Stéphane Symons

Ludwig Binswanger and Fernand Deligny on the Human Condition

Wandering Lines

palgrave
macmillan

Stéphane Symons
Institute of Philosophy
University of Leuven
Leuven, Belgium

ISBN 978-3-031-66122-8   ISBN 978-3-031-66123-5   (eBook)
https://doi.org/10.1007/978-3-031-66123-5

ACKNOWLEDGMENTS

Many thanks to Roland Breeur, Johanna Cockx, Thibault Desmet, Jan Masschelein, Paul Moyaert, Johannes Muselaers, Greet Van Thienen, and the editorial team at Palgrave Macmillan. Thanks also to publisher L'Arachnéen (Sandra Alvarez de Toledo) and Thierry Boccon-Gibod for the permission to publish some photos from Fernand Deligny's archive.

This essay originated in the project G030023N: The Frankfurt School meets Phenomenology (funded by the Research-Council Flanders) and the project C14/18/048: Space Thought and Taught (funded by BOF KUL).

CONTENTS

LIST OF FIGURES

CHAPTER 1

Introduction

Abstract The introduction explores the concept of unrealized possibilities in life and history, often framed as "what-if" questions. It briefly discusses the impact of these questions on individual lives and collective historical events. The text also introduces the works of psychiatrists and philosophers Ludwig Binswanger and Fernand Deligny, contrasting their approaches to psychiatry. Binswanger's theoretical humanism is juxtaposed with Deligny's more poetic and artistic approach. The introduction examines the paradoxes in Binswanger's case study of *Ellen West* and Deligny's descriptions of *Janmari*. The exploration of unrealized possibilities in these cases provides unique insights into their lives and treatments.

Keywords Alternate history • Hans Blumenberg • Ludwig Binswanger • Fernand Deligny • Unrealized possibilities

In August 1915, when British, French, Australian, and New Zealand troops have been trying for months to capture the Gallipoli Peninsula from the Ottoman enemy, the American magazine *The Atlantic Monthly* publishes a poem by forty-one-year-old poet Robert Frost. At first glance, the famous "The Road Not Taken" is

S. Symons, *Ludwig Binswanger and Fernand Deligny on the Human Condition*, https://doi.org/10.1007/978-3-031-66123-5_1

completely unrelated to developments on the world stage but it will soon capture the hearts of many readers. In their view, Frost articulates the awareness that in human existence many opportunities will inevitably remain untapped. "Two roads diverged in a yellow wood/And sorry I could not travel both/And be one traveler, long I stood/And looked down one as far as I could/To where it bent in the undergrowth/Then took the other, as just as fair."

The course of our lives could indeed have been completely different if we had made a different choice at specific moments. Moreover, it is hard to deny that many essential decisions are the result of a coincidence. What would have become of me if, many years ago, I had left unanswered that e-mail from a woman at the time unknown to me? Would I have met the love of my life? And how would my life have turned out if, looking for a job, I had not struck up a conversation with that acquaintance who pointed out an open position at the university? Would I have ever secured the job of my dreams? But also: would I have survived if I had taken the subway at Brussels' Maelbeek metro station a few hours later on March 22, 2016? And what would have happened if I hadn't been able to duck just in time for that passing car last week?

Certainly, the "what-if?" question has something noncommittal about it. It seems like a waste of time, something for a lazy Sunday afternoon when you are feeling slightly off. It confronts with events that can't be undone anyway, so why bother? Yet such a question gives color to the uniqueness of each life story. What seems on the surface to be just a useless thought experiment can help focus on what matters most. A brief detour along the unrealized possibilities of your life then culminates in a more rooted awareness of who, and what, one has effectively become. Thus the "what-if?" question can still make a real difference somewhere. It can make you grateful for family happiness and professional opportunities or breathe a sigh of relief because of dodged misfortune. It can elicit frustration at the opportunities you let slip through the fingers but just as easily exhort you to do things differently in the future.

Such a sense of unrealized possibility can also overwhelm you when you shift your gaze from your own unique life path to the level of collective, historical events. The aforementioned 1915 Battle of Gallipoli, for example, could as well *not have* happened. These fights turned into a nightmare for the Entente powers. More than half a year after this battle began, the British, French, Australian, and New Zealand soldiers had to withdraw again from the region, abandoning for good their ambition to take the Ottoman capital of Constantinople. Meanwhile, the battle had claimed tens of thousands of lives. The withdrawal of the allies would give a huge boost to the nationalist feeling of the Turkish people. It lay directly at the origins of the Turkish War of Independence (1919–1923) and the founding of Turkey eight years later. Nevertheless, many historians have since agreed that even this important historical event could have been avoided, provided a little more military acumen on the part of the Allies. Failing supplies and armaments, an unfavorable geographical context and a lack of experience are just some of the explanations for the failure of the Entente forces. They are largely factors that an ingenious strategist could have predicted. Indeed, several important generals, including the commander-in-chief of the French army, Joseph Jacques Césaire Joffre, *had* actually predicted the failure of this operation. They had explicitly advised from the start of this military operation not to open a front in Gallipoli. According to them, all attention had to go to the Western front.[1] Never will anyone know with certainty what would have happened if Joffre had won the argument—whether World War I would not already have ended much earlier, and with less bloodshed, by the concentration of all military efforts in Western Europe. Perhaps even the relationship between the EU and today's Turkey would have looked completely different?

When the "what-if?" question focuses on the collective level of history, it certainly loses its non-committal nature. It now probes events that have had an impact on a huge number of human lives. Carefully identifying the decisive moments at which history took

---

[1] John Keegan, *The First World War* (London: Pimlico, 1999), 255.

one particular direction rather than another increases our scholarly grasp of a shared past. Such a thought exercise rises far above the indeterminate, subjective feeling of seized and missed opportunities. It deepens our knowledge of objective facts. Historical "what-if?" scenarios are therefore found fodder for a lot of literary authors. In recent decades, so-called *alternate histories* have become a veritable genre. These are descriptions of *what might have been but was not*. For example, Philip Roth wrote an alternate history in which the populist, anti-Semitic, and xenophobic ex-pilot Charles Lindbergh is elected president of the United States in 1940 (*The Plot Against America*), Philip K. Dick explored a world order in which not the Allies but the Axis powers won the Second War (*The Man in the High Castle*), and Stephen Fry, for his part, explored what might have happened had Adolf Hitler never been born (*Making History*). As far-fetched as these stories may be, they did refine our historical consciousness. Some figures of the past were magnified in them, while others were deleted from history in their entirety. That the resulting plotlines feel so *unreal* makes us dwell even more on the past *as it was*. Moreover, this perspective on a (non-real) past sheds a very unique light on today's world. For the fact that these authors have talked about (alternative) history is explained in part by their dissatisfaction with certain developments in the present. They deploy the historical "what-if?" question as a warning against specific dangers from contemporary society and politics, not least the increased tendency toward totalitarianism. In this way, too, the exploration of unrealized possibilities can tell us something about an all too undeniable reality.

Somewhere between a highly individual reflection on one's own life and an objectifiable description of reality, that's where one can find philosophy and philosophical reflection. Indeed, philosophical thinking is akin both to a subjectively colored thought experiment and to the search for a neutral perspective on the world. It allows itself to be fed by seemingly non-committal exercises of thought but reaches out for forms of irrefutable knowledge. It demands support from logical inferences, clear arguments, and factual certainties but should nevertheless take into account its somewhat obscure origins: rational, philosophical thinking has in many cases emerged from emotional self-examination and intense, personal experiences. Because of this interweaving of the individual and the universal, philosophy also falls prey to the lure of the "what-if?" question. This is nicely expressed in the book *Die Sorge geht über den Fluß* by the German cultural philosopher Hans Blumenberg (1920–1996). In it he devotes a chapter to what he calls *Verfehlungen*, a German word that should literally be translated as "shortcomings" and resonates with "negligence" but in this context refers to "failed encounters" or "missed opportunities."[2] Blumenberg gives a host of examples of such "failed encounters" between legendary artists, leading writers, and important philosophers. For example, the glorious Greek artist Apelles (fourth century B.C.) wanted to visit the equally famous artist Protogenes but missed him twice because Protogenes turned out not to be at home. As a memento of his two visits, Apelles each time drew a colored line on Protogenes' board, who himself added a third colored line. Or there is the no less mythical "conversation" between the two most important literary authors of the twentieth century, Marcel Proust and James Joyce. When they finally met in 1922, Proust would not have gotten beyond asking, "Do you like to eat truffles?" to which Joyce would have replied to him, "Yes, I like them very much." And what of the "meeting" between the two giants of early, analytic philosophy, Ludwig Wittgenstein and Gottlob Frege? A nervous Wittgenstein knocked on the door of Frege's residence in Jena but was evidently so disappointed by the outward appearance of the man who appeared in the doorway that at that moment nothing but the word "impossible!" crossed his lips. It is tempting to reduce these "failed encounters" to meaningless anecdotes. The facts about Apelles and Protogenes, Proust and Joyce, and Wittgenstein and Frege seem trivial and they do not contribute anything to the interpretation of their work. Rather, they spill over into, indeed, the "what-if?" question: what brilliant works of art, literary

---

[2] Hans Blumenberg, *Die Sorge geht über den Fluß* (Frankfurt-am-Main: Suhrkamp Verlag, 1987), 169–193.

masterpieces, or profound insights might have resulted from an *artistic* collaboration between Apelles and Protogenes, a *literary* conversation between Proust and Joyce, and a *philosophical* discussion between Wittgenstein and Frege? Yet Blumenberg finds this background information extremely relevant. According to him, it illustrates that the artworks of Apelles and Protogenes, the books of Proust and Joyce, and the philosophical theses of Wittgenstein and Frege are not separate from everyday life. They are the fruit of *human activity* and prove that works of genius and ideas do not descend upon us like manna from heaven. They show that even the most impactful artists, writers, and philosophers are above all *individuals*, with idiosyncrasies and mishaps, insecurities and ego-issues. Therefore, Blumenberg stresses that it is precisely in these *missed* opportunities that something essential is expressed. For example, he points out that the artwork that resulted from the three lines of Apelles and Protogenes was little later included as a masterpiece in Caesar's collection, subsequently embraced by Renaissance artists, and to this day can be considered a distant precursor of non-figurative art. The conversation between Proust and Joyce was also far from banal, according to Blumenberg. The anecdote about Proust's curiosity about Joyce's food preferences would either refer to a polite way of breaking the ice and countering assertiveness, or indicate a deliberate twisting of the facts by Joyce, and this in order to ridicule Proust. In either case, then, the conversation between the two literary giants would have revolved around much more than a culinary delicacy. And Wittgenstein's disappointment with Frege's outward appearance would in turn have foreshadowed his later inability to appreciate Wittgenstein's philosophical ideas. In short, according to Blumenberg, these encounters were not nearly as "failed" as one might think. For the very reason that these opportunities were "missed," they tell us something unexpected and meaningful about the protagonists' worlds of thought and life. These "failed encounters" bring us an insight that might not have surfaced as such in a "successful" conversation.

This little book is also devoted to such a philosophical *Verfehlung*. A first protagonist is the Swiss psychiatrist and philosopher Ludwig

Binswanger (1881–1966). The nephew of Otto Ludwig Binswanger, who was once Friedrich Nietzsche's therapist, he was born into a wealthy family of intellectuals and psychiatrists. When he took over the helm from his father Robert Binswanger in 1911 and took office as director of the Bellevue sanatorium in Kreuzlingen, Ludwig transformed the hospital into a care facility that, above all, searched for "the *human being* in psychiatry." In his acclaimed novel *The Radetzsky March* (1932), Austrian writer Joseph Roth describes Bellevue as "a hospital where cautious but pricey care was given to insane people of wealthy origins who were used to being pampered and treated by the nurses with the gentleness of a midwife."[3] Under Binswanger's directorship, Bellevue indeed grows into a care facility for the *rich and famous*, with such notorious residents as the dancer Vaslav Nijinsky and the expressionist painter Ernst Ludwig Kirchner. Each patient is promised customized care, with room for one-on-one counseling and an application of the latest insights from theoretical psychiatry.

A second protagonist in this "failed encounter" is the French educator, philosopher, poet, and filmmaker Fernand Deligny (1913–1996). All his life, Deligny devoted himself to so-called "alternative" psychiatry. Working for institutions in Armentières (1939–1943), La Grande Cordée (1948–1962), and La Borde (1965–1967), he wanted to challenge the disciplining mechanisms of classical medical science from within. In 1967, he goes one step further. He exchanges the search for an alternative form of psychiatry for something much more radical: he wants to mobilize the whole of society as a caregiver.[4] This can only happen through a new "network" that, unlike a psychiatric institution, "interweaves

---

[3] Joseph Roth, *Radetzkymarsch* (Amsterdam: Allert de Lange, 1975), 236–237.

[4] For an excellent discussion of the life and work of Fernand Deligny, see Catherine Perret, *Le tacite, l'humain. Anthropologie politique de Fernand Deligny* (Paris: Éditions du Seuil, 2021). My exposition of the notions of "milieu" and "gesture" (cf. infra) rely on Perret's interpretation. See also Igor Krtolica, "La tentative des Cévennes. Deligny et la question de l'institution," *Chimères* 1, 72 (2010), 73–97.

itself with reality as it is, in circumstances as they are."[5] Deligny will later describe such a network as a "life raft" and a "spider web" and builds it out in a small village in southern France. There, until the end of his life, he takes in autistic children from all walks of life.

As far as is known, Binswanger and Deligny never met. Unlike the "failed encounters" of Apelles and Protogenes, Proust and Joyce, and Wittgenstein and Frege, they did not effectively interact. So there are no amusing anecdotes about faltering conversations or clashing egos to recover from the past. Moreover, when Deligny settles down in southern France and establishes his own healthcare network, Binswanger has been dead for more than a year. Any conversation between Binswanger and Deligny is therefore purely fictional, and no one will ever know what would have been said in fact. Neither did they refer to each other's works or ideas. Still, it is worthwhile to bring Binswanger and Deligny together in these pages, especially starting from Blumenberg's suggestion that it is precisely the *absence* of a substantive conversation that can at times be so revelatory. In the case of Binswanger and Deligny, there are at least two good reasons for this. First, in order to put our finger on Binswanger's theoretical work we do well to contrast it with a completely different frame of mind—a frame of mind so far removed from Binswanger's that no real dialogue would even have been possible between the two. Deligny's work will therefore serve as a contrasting fluid to hold Binswanger's psychiatric theory up to the light in a new way. Indeed, from the awareness of a "missed conversation" with Deligny, we will be able to better grasp the extent to which Binswanger's approach in Kreuzlingen was founded on humanistic, existentialist, and phenomenological assumptions of a purely abstract and conceptual nature. Deligny's oeuvre has a rather poetic and artistic slant, and he was loath to accept Binswanger's ambition to turn psychiatry into a conclusive *theory*, with all the generalizing knowledge claims that this entails. Precisely because

---

[5] Fernand Deligny, "Paroles, geste, silence," in *Oeuvres*, ed. Sandra Alvarez de Toledo (Paris: L'Arachnéen, 2017), 705. See also idem, *L'Arachnéen et autres textes (Paris: L'*Arachnéen, 2008).

Deligny's project was so *opposed* to Binswanger's, we will be able to better analyze Binswanger's philosophical beliefs.

There is a second rationale for giving space to an imaginary conversation between Binswanger and Deligny, even though in reality such a conversation would perhaps have been unfruitful. Their "failed encounter" brings out a huge paradox at the core of at least one of Binswanger's case studies, that of *Ellen West*: Binswanger's embrace of an abstract-theoretical and philosophical humanism did not prevent him from describing his patient *Ellen* as a nonhuman, purely thing-like entity. The humanist, existentialist, and phenomenological theories that captured Binswanger's interest invariably dealt with the irreplaceability of each individual. Each person is deemed to be unique and to stand in the world in his or her very own way. Moreover, Binswanger's humanism stresses that each person, in freedom and independence, can deal with the finiteness of existence. In his accounts of *Ellen*'s treatment, however, Binswanger quickly made it clear that, in his view, this form of humanity did not apply to her. He seemed convinced that no lived self-consciousness was possible. Therefore, soon after *Ellen*'s admission in Bellevue, he made a crushing diagnosis that melted away any hope of recovery. When she committed suicide immediately after her discharge from Bellevue, there was no way that this could have been avoided, according to her therapist.

How different is the situation in Deligny's descriptions of *Janmari*, one of the severely autistic and mutistic youngsters he took under his wing for many years in his "network" in southern France. Deligny saw *Janmari*'s behavior as thoroughly "human." His actions, movements, and gestures were at times downright estranging, but Deligny nevertheless discovered in them a unique ability to interact with the living environment. According to him, *Janmari* embodied an exceptional life force that had done away with all reflections on death and finitude. To arrive at this observation, Deligny did not need the conceptual backing of a purely abstract humanism. Indeed, he made any form of philosophical humanism suspect. Because it seeks to define man by a well-circumscribed essence (language, rationality, socialization), any philosophical humanism, according to Deligny, inevitably results in a mechanism of exclusion. For if the concept of "human being" is fleshed out from the ability to talk, think rationally, or build meaningful relationships with others, what do you call a boy who has never talked, is cognitively limited, and barely wants to interact with others? From Deligny's perspective, the paradox underlying Binswanger's case study of *Ellen West* is particularly sobering: the Swiss psychiatrist would be believed to have applied his theoretical humanism too *much* rather than too *little* in his therapeutic practice. Consequently, Deligny's oeuvre can be read as a reckoning with Binswanger's existentialist and phenomenological conceptual apparatus.

But the true protagonists of this story are *Ellen* and *Janmari*. Not much is known about either of them. It is certain that they never met: the tragic death of *Ellen* took place many years before the birth of *Janmari*. Yet this booklet seeks to shape an *alternate history* in which both people could have met. Of course, *Ellen*'s sad fate is not undone when one wonders what might have happened had she been included in Deligny's "network," together with *Janmari*, and not dropped off by her husband at Binswanger's Bellevue. And it is equally impossible, and improper, to pass judgment on a therapist's actions and decisions from a safe, historical distance and without much factual information. Asking whether *Ellen could have benefited* from Deligny's approach is therefore in no way tantamount to claiming that Binswanger's treatment involved a *Verfehlung* in the common sense of that word: a negligence. On this no one can or should make any straightforward claims. But from an imaginary confrontation between Binswanger and Deligny, and an equally imaginary meeting between *Ellen* and *Janmari*, at least one thing becomes clear: a different therapeutic approach would indeed have been possible.

CHAPTER 2

Ellen

Abstract This chapter focuses on the life of a patient, referred to as *Ellen West*, who suffered from severe eating disorders and mental health issues in the early twentieth century. It explores her struggle with her body image and her desire to be "soft and ethereal," leading to a life dominated by the fear of gaining weight and an insatiable hunger. The document discusses the psychiatric approaches of Ludwig Binswanger and other influential psychiatrists of the time, highlighting their diagnosis of *Ellen*'s condition as severe schizophrenia and "autism." Despite their efforts, *Ellen*'s condition worsens, leading to her eventual suicide. The chapter explores Binswanger's existential psychiatry, focusing on his concepts of being-in-the-world, self, and embodiment. It critically examines his humanistic perspective and his belief in the individual's ability to construct a unique "inner life history." The chapter concludes with a discussion on the paradoxical interweaving of life and death in *Ellen*'s case, as seen through Binswanger's lens.

Keywords Binswanger • *Ellen West* • Existential psychiatry • Phenomenology • Being-in-the-world • Self • Embodiment • Death

S. Symons, *Ludwig Binswanger and Fernand Deligny on the Human Condition*, https://doi.org/10.1007/978-3-031-66123-5_2

On January 14, 1921, a new patient rings the bell at the Bellevue sanatorium in Kreuzlingen. The 32-year-old woman is in bad shape. For more than a decade she has suffered from a compulsive fear of gaining weight. At the same time, she has an insatiable hunger. She longs to devour food like a wild animal does. Consequently, this happens more and more often. At such times, the woman says she throws herself on her meals like a ravenous predator, only to swallow enormous amounts of laxatives afterward, consumed by anxiety. With those pills, she maintains the desire to be "*soft and ethereal*" and even "bodiless."[1] After all these years, such internal conflicts have triggered a severe depression, with the thought of suicide also becoming more frequent. Moreover, her illness has taken a heavy physical toll: when she registered in Kreuzlingen, her body weight had dropped to around 43 kilograms.

During her stay in the sanatorium, her behavior remains unchanged. She feels like a "*dead body among living human beings*" and suffers from a sense of total futility.[2] The medical report of her stay in Kreuzlingen reveals that she is, literally and figuratively, *stuck*. Her "life story no longer leads as a *road* to the future." Rather, it has become a "*circle*, in a present closed off from the future and dominated by the past, and therefore empty." This is reflected in the way the patient moves physically and relates to the space that surrounds her. The patient "does not walk somewhere a little further, only to return ... but she (merely) stumbles on and yet turns in circles." The woman evokes "the image of the lioness trapped in the cage, circling along the bars, searching in vain for a way out. If we want to translate this image into an existential expression, it must read like this: hell."[3] The renowned psychiatrist Emil Kraepelin who comes to examine her in Bellevue puts forward the diagnosis of melancholy. Ludwig Binswanger, the director of the institution, suggests schizophrenia

---

[1] Ludwig Binswanger, "Der Fall Ellen West," in *Ausgewählte Werke. Band 4. Der Mensch in der Psychiatrie*, ed. Alice Holzhey-Kunz (Heidelberg: Roland Asanger Verlag, 1994), 76.

[2] Ibid., 100.

[3] Ibid., 118–119.

accompanied by anorexia and bulimia. With such intense symptoms and such a severe diagnosis, recovery is out of the question, according to both doctors. They are not surprised that the patient's condition becomes more worrisome by the day. After about three months, the risk of suicide is estimated to be so high that a stay in the open ward of the sanatorium no longer seems justified. Around this time, Binswanger contacts his influential colleagues Eugen Bleuler and Alfred Hoche for extra expertise. It is Bleuler who, in 1911, coined the term "autism," thereby designating the schizophrenic condition of turning away from painful realities and replacing them with a purely internal life of hallucinations and fantasies. Convinced that this description matches the emotional state of his patient very well, Binswanger does not hold back in calling her condition one of "autism."[4] Hoche, for his part, had made a name for himself a year earlier through a notorious publication in which he, together with the jurist Karl Binding, argued for the right to kill human beings whose life "is unworthy of living."[5] When both psychiatrists confirm Binswanger's diagnosis of severe schizophrenia, the situation does indeed become completely hopeless. "The therapeutic usefulness of internment is now clearly rejected."[6] On March 30, the woman leaves the care facility with her husband. A brief sense of relief soon gives way to a severe breakdown. The symptoms are now even more pronounced than during her stay in Kreuzlingen, and reuniting with family is harder on her than expected. On the third day after her return home, for the first time in a long while, the woman feels satisfied after her meal. She reads a bit, takes a walk, and writes letters. Yet that same evening she takes a high dose of poison, ending her young life.

* * *

[4] Ibid., 203.

[5] Karl Binding and Alfred Hoche, *Die Freigabe der Vernichtung lebensunwerten Lebens: ihr Maß und ihre Form* (Leipzig: Meiner, 1922). In the late 1930s, this book will become an important inspiration for the Nazi program of involuntary euthanasia, Aktion T4.

[6] Binswanger, "Der Fall Ellen West", 103–104.

Today, more than a hundred years after her death, we still do not know her name. It was Ludwig Binswanger who wrote out her history as a leading case study. He did this in 1944, more than twenty years after meeting her in Kreuzlingen and gave her the fictional name *Ellen West*, after the character Rebecca West from Ibsen's play "Rosmersholm." Binswanger himself has always remained a famous name, though. He is chronicled as a founder of existential psychiatry and an influential and erudite scholar. In his extensive work, he draws attention to the ability of each individual to build an inner cohesive "spiritual life" through the reconciliation of apparent contradictions and mental conflicts. According to him, each person is characterized by their own "inner life history." This inner life, unfolding in time, consists of a series of lived experiences, which are woven together into the unbroken whole that gives form and color to a truly unique and irreplaceable existence. "(O)ur interest is … in … the unique, temporal sequence of the contents of lived experience." That life path points to "the individual spiritual person" and is "the origin or core of all experience, in short, *the inner history of the person's life.*"[7] The unique essence of an individual is thus not a predetermined fact, since it is constructed from the many events that occur in a life. Binswanger argues that the task of psychology is to retrieve the unique, inner, and spiritual essence built up in each life trajectory, as each individual is characterized by a "motivational structure" that gives coherence and substance to a set of mental impulses and desires. "In the inner history of life the inner 'core' of a person, their spiritual person, flourishes and develops, and conversely it is from this history, and only from it, that we come to know the spiritual person."[8]

Both in Binswanger's practice and in his philosophical-theoretical oeuvre, this exploration of the inner life of each individual results in

[7] Ludwig Binswanger, "Lebensfunktion und innere Lebensgeschichte," in *Ausgewählte Werke. Band 3. Vorträge und Aufsätze*, ed. Max Herzog (Heidelberg: Roland Asanger Verlag, 1992), 81.

[8] Ibid., 85. See also, among others, idem, "Über Phänomenologie," in *Ausgewählte Werke. Band 3. Vorträge und Aufsätze*, 35–69.

an emphatically humanistic perspective. It is this perspective, and the vision of the human being that underlies it, that is central to the first part of this essay. It provides the framework for a *Daseinsanalyse*, that is, for Binswanger's idiosyncratic interweaving of psychiatry, phenomenology, and existentialism. Binswanger searches for the mysteries of human existence and explores the many ways in which an individual relates to the world, to other individuals, and to the finitude of life. Emphasizing the centrality and uniqueness of the human being, he also seeks to interpret symptoms as dynamic responses to external events. Therefore, they should not be reduced to mere dysfunctions. According to Binswanger, "the sick person is in a sense closer to the Dasein than we are—even if they are caught in a veritable dizziness of this Dasein."[9] Pathological behavior is above all the expression of the patient's "inner life history" rather than a series of signs to be deciphered or a constellation of physical ailments. In Binswanger's view, the mental universe and physical behavior of the patient testify to a power and dynamic all their own. They should not be studied merely as symptoms but as functions of life and thus, at all times, as a human reaction to external events. "Instead of considering their relation to other abnormal psychological phenomena and the conditions for their emergence, (*Daseinsanalysis*) looks only for the characteristic signs immanent to this psychopathological lived experience that can be discovered in it. Thus the personal background visibly comes to the fore in every lived experience that takes place; or, in other words, in every particular lived experience the experiencer reveals something of themselves; through every lived experience we see through the *experiencer*."[10] Binswanger's psychiatric therapy is therefore primarily focused on the recovery and expression of the "spiritual core" hidden in the patient's psychological distress. Committed to rebuilding the coherence of the patient's mental state, the therapist helps them, above all, to regain the ability to say "I."

---

[9] Ludwig Binswanger, quoted in Georges Didi-Huberman, *L'image survivante. Histoire de l'art et temps des fantômes selon Aby Warburg* (Paris: Les Éditions de Minuit, 2002), 386.

[10] Binswanger, "Über Phänomenologie," 68.

"The essence of psychopathological phenomena is that they never stand alone, but always take place in the background of an ego, of a person, or in other words, we always see them as an expression or a manifestation emanating from this or that person."[11] Through this reconstruction of a spiritual unity, however fragile and momentary, conflicts and contradictions can give way to the ongoing series of "lived experiences" that are supposed to constitute a stable self.

This humanistic frame of mind shows great optimism: in theory, one should be able to help every patient. For even the most ill patient is above all a *human being* and can in principle still lead a meaningful existence. One would therefore expect Binswanger to consider someone untreatable and incurable in only the rarest of cases. Yet this is exactly what happens when in April 1921 it is revealed that *Ellen's* mental condition has remained unchanged after months of internment. In his abstract-theoretical texts, the founder of existential psychiatry may well associate a human life with seemingly infinite possibilities, yet he ascribes to the concrete individual *Ellen* an unattainable "*Todgeweihtheit.*"[12] In his own view, Binswanger has several well-founded reasons for this. *Ellen's* diaries indeed reveal a clear desire to die. She writes: "Death is the greatest happiness in our lives, though not the only one. Without hope of the end, existence would be unbearable. Only the certainty that sooner or later the end will come gives me some comfort."[13] *Ellen's* "life history," according to Binswanger, is rather a "death history" and can be called downright "tragic." In *Ellen's* case, life is fully cast over by its *end*. The thought of death is animated with an almost saving power. In *Ellen's* existence, according to Binswanger, the thought of death does "*nothing* but give joy, give strength, feed hope, awaken love, and enlighten her spirit."[14] "Death is here longed for as the climax of a *festive*

---

[11] Ibid., 58.
[12] Binswanger, "Der Fall Ellen West," 116.
[13] *Ellen*, quoted in ibid., 78.
[14] Binswanger, "Der Fall Ellen West," 132.

existence."[15] It is striking that Binswanger's *own* position is entirely in line with that of his patient. He does not seem to find it at all surprising, let alone shocking, that a patient experiences death as a liberating and even celebratory event. On the contrary, Binswanger agrees with his patient that her self-chosen death represents an ultimate, and posthumous, victory. "The human being now moves in a circulus vitiosus, it is the snake biting its own tail. But because she is still able to 'think of herself,' in freely chosen death, she is ultimately able to break this circle, she is still able to crush the head of the snake. That is the victory of this existence over the power of 'hell.'"[16] For this reason, Binswanger repeats no less than seventeen times that *Ellen*'s suicide is "authentic." It is not the sad illustration of unfathomable human suffering, nor proof that his therapeutic approach has failed. Rather, according to Binswanger, this suicide demonstrates that even "Nothingness" can have a "positivity" and that death, too, can give "clarity" and "meaning" to life. *Ellen* had become "ripe for her death" and death fell into her lap like "a ripe fruit." Binswanger thus sees *Ellen*'s death not as *opposed* to her life, but as "the necessary fulfillment of the meaning of life in this existence."[17]

*   *   *

Such a surprising interweaving between life and death needs further elaboration and conceptual foundation. Binswanger underpins the theoretical framework for his *Daseinsanalyse* with at least three philosophical concepts: world, self, and body. He borrows these three concepts largely from Edmund Husserl and Martin Heidegger and deploys them as a philosophical justification for his aforementioned

[15] Ibid., 123.
[16] Ibid., 198.
[17] Ibid., 133–134.

humanistic project.[18] As "existentials," they describe the basic functions of a meaningful, human existence. As a result, according to
Binswanger, they also set out the most important lines for successful
therapy. In his view, a patient is only truly helped when they recover
the lived connection to the world, regain the stability of their "I,"
and experience their own body as the natural connection between
these two different realities. These three concepts also play a crucial
role in the case study about *Ellen,* but in a purely negative way.
Binswanger views *Ellen*'s situation as hopeless because each of these
three existential functions is disrupted by her autism and schizophrenia. *Ellen*'s behavior, therefore, refers primarily to an *existential*
problem and cannot be adequately understood with a merely psychological vocabulary: "The fear of gaining weight ... (is) *equally an*
expression of the fear of the confinement and shrinkage of her
existence."[19] In Binswanger's view, *Ellen* leads a dehumanized,
"empty," and, in the final analysis, *dead* existence, and this because
she no longer possesses the meaning-giving faculties that make a
humane life possible: "A person who wants to lead such a humanly
impossible existence is rightly and justifiably called *crazy.*"[20]

---

[18] This intellectual influence does not mean that Binswanger's project was fully
endorsed by the phenomenologists that he drew inspiration from. Heidegger, for
one, was very critical of Binswanger's project on account of the overall absence of
ontological concerns (for Heidegger the analysis of the human subject and their
interactions with the world is ultimately dependent on the question, and disclo-
sure, of Being) and the conflation of the concepts care and love (for the latter
concept Binswanger primarily drew from Max Scheler). For an analysis of this
discussion, and Heidegger's Zollikon seminars, see Francesca Brencio, "Heidegger
and Binswanger: Just a Misunderstanding?", *The Humanistic Psychologist* 43
(2015), 278–296 and Anthony Vincent Fernandez, "Beyond the Ontological
Difference: Heidegger, Binswanger and the Future of Existential Analysis," in
Existential Medicine: Essays on Health and Illness, ed. K. Aho (New York: Rowman
and Littlefield International, 2018), 27–42.

[19] Binswanger, "Der Fall Ellen West,", 129.

[20] Ibid., 182.

First, Binswanger emphasizes the importance of an intentional orientation toward an "outside." Here he assumes that meaningful interaction with our environment can only come from a coherent being-in-the-world. Our internal mental life or *idios kosmos* is by definition non-shared (individual) but it is inextricably linked to a *koinos kosmos* or *koinonia* that is also inhabited by others and shaped together with them. Only from this orientation to an outside, and to others, is it avoided that the experience of our environment degenerates into solipsism, and thereby culminates in fragmentation and anxiety. The therapist must guard the patient from any tendency to isolate themselves from their environment and is supposed to help the patient discover that their mental state, even during illness, offers a unique perspective on an external world. In the case of eccentricity, for example, "what we call psychotherapy is essentially no more than an attempt to bring the patient to a point where they can 'see' how the totality of human existence or 'being-in-the-world' is structured and to see at which of their nodes they have gone beyond himself. That is, the goal of psychotherapy is to bring the patient out of their eccentricity and safely 'back to earth.' Only from this point is a new *departure* and a new *ascent* possible."[21] Binswanger makes use of Heraclitus' famous statement that "[t]he waking have *one* and the same world in common; in sleep each returns to his own world" to indicate that the therapist's task is to "awaken" the patient and set them on their way to a shared world.[22] Binswanger contrasts the patient's unhealthy urge to "lose themselves in pure subjectivity" with their ability to reopen to a social and communal universe. The patient's search for an entirely "other" universe can only make the

---

[21] Ludwig Binswanger, "Drei Formen missglückten Daseins," in *Ausgewählte Werke. Band 1. Formen mißglückten Daseins*, ed. Max Herzog (Heidelberg: Roland Asanger Verlag, 1992), 247. See also Ludwig Binswanger, 'Über Ideenflucht', in ibidem., 151.

[22] Heraclitus, quoted in Ludwig Binswanger, "Traum und Existenz," in *Ausgewählte Werke. Band 3. Vorträge und Aufsätze*, 113.

therapist "wince" because "the meaning of life is always something transsubjective, something universal, 'objective' and impersonal."[23]

Binswanger argues, however, that *Ellen* has undone all ties to the shared world, thereby creating for herself an entirely "other," purely subjective, and strictly personal universe. Indeed, she herself confesses that she is "completely isolated in a glass ball." "I see the people through a glass wall, their voices sounding muffled to me. I long unspeakably to join them. I shout, but they do not hear. I stretch out my arms to them; but my hands only bump against the walls of my glass sphere."[24] In addition to this *social* isolation, *Ellen* suffers from *spatial* isolation. Her body, too, according to Binswanger, has become "enclosed," and not only because, as described earlier, it often remains trapped in circular motion.[25] Whereas a humane existence presupposes a *gestimmte* (emotionally colored), shared space beholden to the individual, *Ellen West*, on the other hand, experiences her living environment as crushingly "external" and inhuman. This spatial isolation goes so far that even the touch of a piece of clothing strikes her body as repulsive. Clothing makes her feel fat but also confronts her with an inescapable and sickening strangeness: "As soon as I feel a pressure on my waist—I mean the pressure of the band of my skirt—my mood darkens; I fall into such a severe depression that it seems like the most terrible tragedy."[26] For these reasons, Binswanger understands *Ellen*'s desire to be soft, ethereal, and bodiless as the complete opposite of a lived, bounded, and rooted human being-in-the-world. It is the symptom of a merely "airy" and "articulate" world, an "infinite desolation," a "nothingness," and a "defective realization."[27] Her social and spatial isolation, according to Binswanger, are proof that she feels

---

[23] Binswanger, "Traum und Existenz," 106.

[24] *Ellen*, quoted in Binswanger, "Der Fall Ellen West," 93.

[25] Ibid., 118.

[26] *Ellen*, quoted in ibid. 87–88. Compare also Ludwig Binswanger, "Das Raumproblem in der Psychopathologie," in *Ausgewählte Werke. Band 3. Vorträge und Aufsätze*, 123–177.

[27] Binswanger, "Der Fall Ellen West," 113–115.

incessantly "threatened" by the outside world and cannot "love" it.[28] The conflict between her two most fundamental desires, the craving for food and the fear of being fat, has made a coherent being-in-the-world impossible. No meaningful interaction with the environment can be created from these fragments.[29]

Whereas Binswanger fills in the notion of being-in-the-world with social and spatial determinations, the concept of self revolves around individuality and temporality. Binswanger understands a human existence as a unique and uninterrupted life-path that runs from the past along the present to the future. A human life is first and foremost an individual, continuous "history" (*Geschichte*) that takes place in time, weaving the past, present, and future into a unique whole. This means that none of these three temporal dimensions should prevail. A lived "now-moment" is always related to, and nourished by, both personal memories of the past and the anticipation of its own, "open" future.[30] Here, too, the therapist has an important role to play. The latter must lead the patient to reconstruct their own life as a "narrative" movement.[31] In this way, crucial phases, changes, and events from the past are linked in a meaningful and subjective way, and the future in turn is charged with a sense of "possibility." Because Binswanger's conceptual framework, like that of Husserl and Heidegger, starts from the unity between self and world, however, a defective being-in-the-world inevitably produces a defective self. "If the world is only a void, the self (physical as well as spiritual) is also only a void; after all, world and self are reciprocal provisions."[32] Those who cannot be oriented toward a shared world are thus just doomed to a fragmentation of their own unique, undivided existential trajectory. Again, according to Binswanger, *Ellen*'s life shows how much can go wrong. Strange as it may sound, this woman, in the eyes of her doctor, misses out on her own self: her life

---

[28] Ibid., 117.
[29] See also ibid., 157.
[30] See Ludwig Binswanger, "Lebensfunktion und innere Lebensgeschichte," 71–94.
[31] Binswanger, "Der Fall Ellen West," 171.
[32] Ibid., 158.

story is really only one of "contradiction" (*Widersinn*) because only a "*not* being herself," and not a "being herself," can still somehow be linked to "meaning" (*Sinn*). *Ellen* is always fleeing from existence; she is running away from her own humanity. In her case, according to Binswanger, we must speak of a "failure of existence."[33] According to Binswanger, *Ellen*'s insatiable hunger is proof of a failure of temporalization and an inability to *develop*. The recurring bouts of eating show a craving for repetition and an "addiction" (*Züchtigkeit*) that condemn the present to the ruthless clasp of a never-vanishing, never-changing, and "dominating" past. Repetition and impeded change determine the temporal structure of addiction: "The addict, deprived of the overarching continuity of their inner life story, *therefore exists only in the moment*, in the moment of apparent fulfillment, not continuously. They live from moment to moment, but are ultimately unsatisfied in every moment."[34] *Ellen* does not have and *is* not a "life history." For her, the present is not a link that blends the past into the future and thereby creates a unique existential trajectory. The now-moment here continues to falter like a broken cogwheel and "stops time."[35]

Because of this internal, temporal fragmentation, according to Binswanger, *Ellen* cannot possibly accept the two most basic existential facts of a human life: birth and death. She fails to give a place to the undeniable "thrownness" and transience of human existence. As a result, Binswanger arrives at a paradoxical conclusion: his patient's entire life may only be lived in the light of the *end* of life, but the *Sein-zum-Tode* (being-toward-death), which should give weight to a human life, is foreign to her. For her, after all, life is not a "design" or "project" that is given substance and color from the realization that one day it will *end* irrevocably. Decisions and choices here are not sharpened by an awareness of human impermanence. On the contrary, according to Binswanger, *Ellen* refuses to resign herself to

---

[33] Ibid., 136.
[34] Ibid., 190.
[35] Ibid., 138.

the limitations of human existence. Because she experiences death only as a *liberation* from life, she lacks the awareness that death and impermanence actually give human existence a *foundation*. In Binswanger's view, *Ellen*'s state of mind is a classic example of Kierkegaardian *despair* or sickness-unto-death: *Ellen* cannot relate to her end of life in a balanced and mature way, and this precisely because she is so obsessed with it. She is *unable to* recognize her raison d'être, and its temporality. As a result, she has fallen into an existential vacuum: she does not "walk away from the ground of her existence—no human being can do that—but she walks into it—like into an abyss. Just as no human being can escape 'their destiny,' can they escape their ground."[36]

Both concepts, "being-in-the-world" and "self," call for a third crucial concept in Binswanger's system of thought: the body or, more correctly, embodiment. Indeed, it is human embodiment that allows a unique self to be involved in a lived way in a shared world: "(T)he body shapes the identity-unit to explain the *world*."[37] The human body is first and foremost an existential body. With this Binswanger does not mean that it is a mere vehicle of our "spiritual core" or an expression of our soul.[38] Indeed, such views assume an artificial distinction between body and spirit. In reality, body and spirit are so inseparable that it no longer makes any sense to place them in opposition to each other. The human being is always involved in the world in both a mental and physical way and can only experience that "outside" as a meaningful environment for that very reason. Consequently, Binswanger points to the distinction between the human body or *Leib* and the not-truly-human corpus or *Körper*. The *Leib* is inherently intertwined with thoughts, feelings, and signification while the *Körper* should just be understood as a non-subjective and therefore purely thing-like reality. "It must always be

---

[36] Ibid., 138.

[37] Ibid., 114.

[38] See Ludwig Binswanger, *Ausgewählte Werke. Band 2. Grundformen und Erkenntnis menschlichen Daseins*, ed. Max Herzog and Hans-Jürg Braun (Heidelberg: Roland Asanger Verlag, 1993), 404.

emphasized that embodiment is not to be confused with the body in the anatomical and anatomico-physiological sense, i.e., the *Körper*, but that this expression (embodiment) must always be understood existentially, i.e., as bodily existence or existence in the body."[39] A *Körper*, on the other hand, cannot be intentionally involved in the world. One of the major points of contention with Freud revolves precisely around this dichotomy between *Leib* and *Körper*. According to Binswanger, Freud disconnects human physicality so much from processes of consciousness and meaning-giving that it is reduced to a mere mechanical, anonymous, and disruptive strangeness, *Körperlichkeit* (corporeality). Binswanger accuses Freud of understanding man primarily as a natural being, driven by internal, instinctual processes. In this way, he risks losing sight of the fact that our embodiment is above all the condition for a thoroughly human and social existence. Freud's naturalistic perspective, according to Binswanger, leads him to regard the relationship with the outside world, and with others, as inherently problematic and in many cases sickening ("Civilization and Its *Dis*contents"). With Freud, then, being in-the-world is by no means the condition of a stable self, existential fulfillment, and a dignified existence. "Freud's concept of homo natura is a scientific construction that is conceivable only if it is based on a destruction of man's experiential knowledge of himself—a destruction, that is, of anthropological experience."[40]

Binswanger's criticism of Freud, however, does not mean that he rejects his concept of the unconscious, or that he questions the link between the unconscious and the body. He too sees unconscious processes, such as dreaming, as inherently intertwined with embodiment. Among other things, he discusses such common dream motifs as falling and flying. In these, embodiment plays an undeniably crucial role. But these dreamed, bodily movements have nothing

---

[39] Binswanger, "Der Fall Ellen West," 122.

[40] Ludwig Binswanger, 'Freuds Auffassung des Menschen im Lichte der Anthropologie' (1936), *Nederlandsch Tijdschrift voor Psychologie*, vol. IV, no. 5 and 6, 285; see also idem., 'Mein Weg zu Freud', in *Ausgewählte Werke. Band 3*, 26 and idem., 'Der Fall Ellen West', 154.

essentially in common with mere *corporeal* (anatomical) movements since they belong to a "matrix of meaning." In a dream, bodily movements like falling and flying, like linguistic expressions and poetic formulas, tell us something essential about our being-in-the-world during the day, and how we experience our own existence. When we say that we "fall from heaven," for example, this does not refer to "a purely corporeal fall (*ein rein körperliches Fallen*), nor to a fall modeled (analogously or metaphorically) after it or derived from it: rather, (this formula) points to an abrupt feeling of disappointment and disgust that the harmony with the world around us and with our fellow human beings, which has hitherto sustained us, has suddenly received a blow that has caused it to falter."[41] For Binswanger, a dream is a "life function" that creates and reveals meaning. A dream is not merely the outlet of anatomical-physical processes. Like the "life history" of the conscious "self," the dream is grounded in *existential* questions: "To show the place of dreaming within the ground (of existence), that was our intention."[42] Thus, contrary to what Freud may claim, biological motivations and instincts, such as eroticism and sexuality, are only "of secondary importance" in dreaming.[43]

Not surprisingly, *Ellen* exemplifies the absolute opposite of a human existence on a bodily level as well. Binswanger sees his patient's body as a mere external *Körper*, just like *Ellen* herself, for that matter. Moreover, according to Binswanger, her body is characterized by a desire to undo itself. It is experienced as a "heaviness" and a "dungeon" and reduces the human being to a thing: "If the expressions 'rusting away' and 'withering away' also have an existential meaning, this is all the more true of 'wearing out', 'becoming a

[41] Binswanger, "Traum und Existenz," 95.

[42] Ibid., 118.

[43] Ibid., 100. Moreover, according to Binswanger, physicality also plays a crucial role in love, but as "transparency" and not as the origin of drives. According to Binswanger, lovers share the feeling of completely appearing to each other, and this is the result of physical gestures or actions such as a wink or kiss. "The 'you-transparency' is an essential part of bodily appearance, and in love all bodily, partial appearances are manifestations of love," in Binswanger, *Grundformen*, 404.

doll and 'merely vegetating'; for here existence is reduced to non-resistance or to sheer passivity, (as in) toys and (what merely) stupidly persists."[44] *Ellen*'s body, as mentioned, stumbles on or goes in circles. One moment it offers the sad spectacle of insatiable greed, only to be consumed afterward by a desire for "shrinkage." Because *Ellen* yearns to be bodiless, she is doomed, according to Binswanger, to experience her own physicality as irreducibly *alien* and even *hostile*. Such an *external* and *borrowed* body is irretrievably lost: it can no longer be spiritually appropriated. "Its own world, the spiritual as well as the physical, is not only experienced as a non-form (*Ungestalt*), but *lives itself out* in this non-form."[45] Any type of lived self-identification falls irrevocably short because mind and body are here opposed as antagonists. With this de-spiritualized and non-subjective physicality, inevitably an existential zero point has been reached.

[44] Binswanger, "Der Fall Ellen West," 117 and 120.
[45] Ibid., 198.

CHAPTER 3

Janmari

Abstract This chapter explores the life and care of Jean-Marie
(*Janmari*), an autistic boy, under Fernand Deligny's innovative
approach in the late 1960s. Deligny, rejecting conventional medical
diagnoses, establishes a supportive community in the Cévennes to
care for *Janmari* and others like him. This network, living closely
with nature and relying on minimal resources, emphasizes sensitivity and openness to the unique behaviors of autistic children.
Deligny develops "maps" to trace the physical movements of these
children, revealing their "wandering lines," which, though seemingly purposeless, demonstrate their capability for interaction and
variation in movement. Deligny's approach contrasts sharply with
traditional psychiatric methods, particularly those of Ludwig
Binswanger, by denying the necessity of a shared language or consciousness of being. Instead, Deligny advocates for a respectful
coexistence, where companions adapt to the children's way of
being, highlighting a fundamentally different yet profoundly human
existence. The chapter concludes with a critical reflection on the
philosophical and therapeutic implications of Deligny's and
Binswanger's methods, suggesting a need to reconsider traditional
views on mental health and patient care.

Keywords Fernand Deligny • *Janmari* • Maps • Drawing •
Movements • Interaction • Wandering lines • Life

Or perhaps not.

I open my laptop and click on a YouTube link. I see a boy of about nineteen years old. He is of average height and has black, sleek hair. He is holding his hands behind his back. He spins in circles, over and over. He does not move a step forward or say a word. In the background I see trees and bushes. Leaves blowing softly in the wind. When the camera zooms out, I see a rocky natural landscape with some old buildings here and there. Some are in dilapidated condition and have no roof. There are sheds with animals, barrels of water, a stone oven for baking bread, a stream. I hear the wind rustling, the birds whistling, the water flowing. And I hear a man's voice: "He spins around/he spins around. Either around himself, the hands/behind the back, one holding the other/ Or while walking as if someone were standing in the middle of his carousel and holding him by the end/of a rope/It is said that it ends badly with a boy/He, he keeps running/towards himself/ That's what the language makes us say/He's running around himself/but if this famous SELF is in fact/absent/empty/this child is running around NOTHING/he's running on nothing/hopelessly/lost/so is it that he's looking for this self/that he's looking for himself?/That's not the way we went/Because with this boy it ended/not well/but also not badly/beyond/beyond/good/and evil."[1] The boy on my computer screen is Jean-Marie J. He has never spoken a word and remains largely indifferent to what is happening around him. But just as suddenly, he is seized by a blind rage that causes him to bang his head against the wall, until he bleeds. He can go for days without eating, only to gorge himself afterward, like a wild and starving animal, on his meal. And at times,

---

[1] Fernand Deligny, "Ce gamin, là," in *Oeuvres*, 1044–1045. The film can be viewed at https://www.youtube.com/watch?v=8Ey8_9j4Zzw.

Fig. 3.1   Still from Ce gamin, là, dir. Renaud Victor (France, 1975)

he keeps going in circles. According to doctors at the renowned La Salpêtrière hospital in Paris, he has autism and encephalopathy (Fig. 3.1).

The film I am watching, *Ce gamin, là*, was shot in the early 1970s. A few years before, in 1967, Jean-Marie was trusted to the care of Fernand Deligny at the age of 12. It is Deligny who gives Jean-Marie the name *Janmari*. He and a group of like-minded people will continue to care for him until his death in 2002. In an unsightly hamlet in Gourgas, in the Gard in the Cévennes, from July 14, 1967 onwards, Deligny brings together like-minded people from all walks of life, ranging from factory workers and teachers to social assistants and unemployed youth. They are not interested in the diagnoses and medical reports of a hospital like La Salpêtrière. Like a spider's web, Deligny's network is thought out to be at once

Fig. 3.2 Fernand Deligny and *Janmari* in the Cévennes, 1973 (photo: Thierry Boccon-Gibod)

agile and strong, demanding an openness and sensitivity to what is *different*. It must be able to weave its way *between* people and things, thus establishing unexpected connections.

For its income, the network relies on Deligny's meager author's salary and free donations. Deligny and his colleagues live side by side, day in and day out, with young people like *Janmari*. They are close to nature and provide for their most basic sustenance themselves (Fig. 3.2).

The first year is hard. In his film, Deligny makes no bones about it. When *Janmari* joins the network in the Cévennes, the verdict of science is merciless: this boy is "incurable/unbearable/unlivable." The words sound like a distant echo from Kreuzlingen in 1921. For a moment, Kraepelin, Bleuler, Hoche, and Binswanger seem to have taken over from Deligny. Their descriptions of *Ellen* involuntarily spring to mind. The terms are repeated several times in the film, like a miserable refrain: "incurable/unlivable."[2] Of course, *Janmari*'s condition is very different from *Ellen*'s, whose diaries and letters illustrate a deep affinity with language and poetry. And the term "autism," used by both *Ellen*'s and *Janmari*'s doctors alike, has in the meanwhile undergone a drastic change. While it was used, in the 1920s, to describe a complex though pathological, internal emotional life, it is, in the 1960s, used to describe the precise opposite: the supposed *absence* of fantasy and *deficiency* of imagination.[3] Still, upon his arrival, *Janmari*'s behavior does bear many similarities to *Ellen*'s when she is dropped off by her husband in Bellevue. He, as well, is termed schizophrenic. *Janmari* also completely isolates himself from his surroundings. He evidently maintains no meaningful relationships with the others, and seems especially in need of repetition and immutability. This is evident from the drawings he makes during those early months. A drawing from December 14, 1967, is full of small circles in pencil. There are many dozens of them, next to and sometimes a bit on top of each other. There will be many more of these drawings the years to come (Fig. 3.3).

The "maps" that Deligny and the companions will later create also point to the same issues. They are the "traces" of *Janmari*'s physical movements on a given day. On the map of a day in September 1967, we see mostly circles and, in Deligny's words, "black flowers," thick black spots to reveal the intense repetition of movement.[4] But the movement maps of 1968, about a year after his

---

[2] Deligny, "Ce gamin, là," 1040.

[3] Bonnie Evans, 'How Autism Became Autism. The Radical Transformation of a Central Concept of Child Development in Britain', *History of the Human Sciences* 26 (3) (2013), 3–31 (https://doi.org/10.1177/0952695113484320).

[4] These maps were actually made only from 1969, but in *Ce gamin, là*, Deligny nevertheless shows a map depicting the situation from September 1967. See also Sandra Alvarez de Toledo, "Introduction et glossaire," in *Cartes et lignes d'erre/ Maps and Wander Lines. Traces du réseau de Fernand Deligny 1969–1979* (Paris: L'Arachnéen, 2013), 1–14.

Fig. 3.3 Tracing made by *Janmari*, 2001–2002 (extract from *Journal de Janmari*, facsimile prepared by Gisèle Durand, Paris: L'Arachnéen, 2013). © Archives Gisèle Durand-Ruiz, courtesy of Editions L'Arachnéen

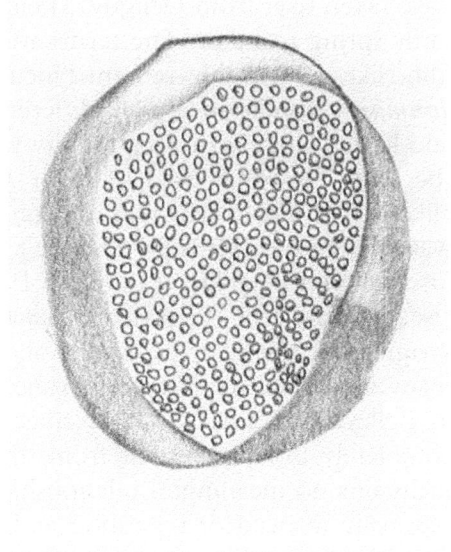

arrival, suddenly look completely different. There are still circles and spots, but the companions now also trace long lines. Deligny will call these lines "*lignes d'erre*," wandering lines. These wandering lines don't go anywhere. They are not functional movements and they have no specific action or process of making as their goal. They show how *Janmari* starts walking around for no obvious reason, stays somewhere, returns to the previous position. There is no meaning or purpose to be found in them. Yet they are of crucial importance to Deligny. He sees *Janmari*'s wandering lines as proof that his physical movements show much more variation than was initially assumed. Moreover, he becomes convinced that *Janmari is* indeed capable of interacting with the outside world, albeit in a very distinct and non-linguistic way: "black flowers/here and there/on the wandering line/here he stopped walking/and the back and forth movement was sometimes less violent/there it is like a scream/and here there is a whisper/but language has nothing to do with it/it is about this back and forth movement/the hands on the back/one holds the other/all those black flowers/are scattered around/sometimes almost imperceptibly/but scattered around nonetheless/the flowers are never completely motionless/and here he vibrates down to his bone marrow/like a divining rod."[5] On the screen, meanwhile, I see images of *Janmari* perched on the side of a river. He is fascinated by the movement of the water and radiates pleasure. Deligny describes how he keeps returning to old and familiar places in the landscape, for example, a crossing of shepherds' paths, a stream, an extinguished fire. They bring him peace and calm him down. *Janmari* also has a strange interest in certain objects, such as a ball of clay with a string, dishes, or a broom. As time goes on, he not only reacts to particular places in the landscape or certain objects but there is also a form of social interaction becoming apparent in his behavior. On the maps, *Janmari*'s wandering lines are now getting closer and closer to those of his companions. Deligny speaks of "*chevêtres*," intersections between the movements of *Janmari* and those of his companions. Though both still live *side by* side, certain gestures and actions of the companions trigger *Janmari*'s interest. When the companions knead dough to bake bread, *Janmari* responds with the same movements, and even splitting a block of wood now goes without a hitch. "July 1969/ something must have happened there/there is still the movement of a clockwork/unchanging/turning in circles/and/moving back and forth/the wheel and the fulcrum/but the wandering line/that follows our TRAJECTS/which are all irrigated by it/does this mean that this boy-here is participating in our PROJECTS?/the idler he was/has now become an extraordinary/machine/capable of anything."[6] For Deligny, it illustrates the success of his "life raft" and "spider web": with the right incentives, even an extremely isolated boy can overcome his fears and anxieties (Fig. 3.4).

*   *   *

---

[5] Deligny, "Ce gamin, là," 1049.
[6] Ibid., 1050.

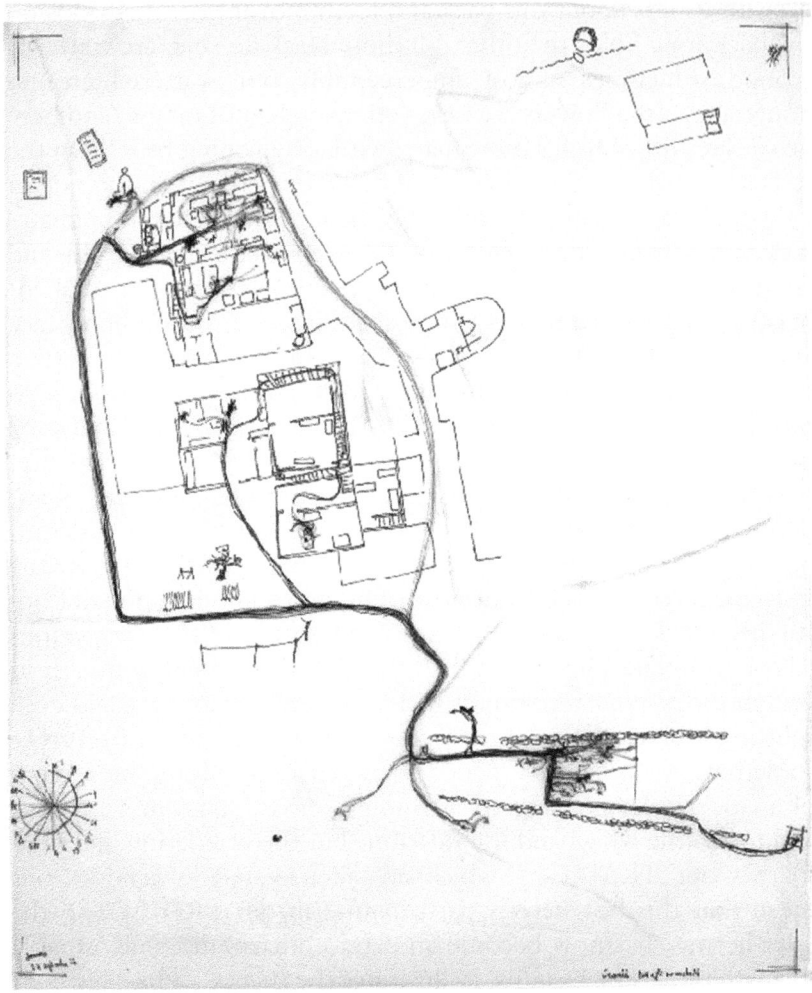

Fig. 3.4 Tracing sheet 11 (*Janmari*'s wandering lines on September 24, 1977, from 6 AM to 6:30 PM), superimposed on bottom tracing sheet 1 (plan of the space), traced by Gisèle Durand-Ruiz and Jacques Lin, Hameau de Graniers, tracing paper, 69 × 59 cm. © Archives Gisèle Durand-Ruiz, courtesy of Editions L'Arachnéen. Photograph: Anaïs Masso

Janmari and *Ellen* received similar diagnoses and share some of the same symptoms. Yet *Janmari*'s story has a very different, and much better ending than *Ellen*'s. Based on that fact, I wonder what Deligny would have thought of Binswanger's conceptual framework and approach, and vice versa, and whether there might not also have been other therapeutic options for a patient like *Ellen*. A therapist obviously cannot be held responsible for the fatal outcome of a history of illness. This also counts for Binswanger, not least because *Ellen* had been suicidal long before she reported to Kreuzlingen. Perhaps *Ellen* was indeed beyond help. If so, no therapeutic approach, including Deligny's, would have made any real difference. Yet it is worth imagining that *Ellen could* also have been treated in a totally different way, and to consider what such treatment might have looked like. It is partly from the perspective of such an *alternate history* that I want to delve further into Deligny's rich oeuvre. No one will ever know what would have happened had Binswanger not seen *Ellen*'s desire for death as something "authentic" and her suicide as a "necessary fulfillment of the meaning of life." But from a purely theoretical confrontation between the views of Binswanger and Deligny, the possibility of a very different therapeutic path does surface. Deligny will at all costs avoid calling anyone's existence "humanly impossible." And doesn't it in any case remain morally problematic to reduce someone's "life history" to a "death history" after only a few months of therapy?

When we compare Deligny's conceptual framework of thought with Binswanger's, many contradictions stand out. Surprisingly, Deligny by no means places the human being at the center of psychiatry. For him, in fact, there is no such thing as a conclusive definition of the human being at all, and the autistic children with whom he lives are fundamentally *different*: "One might think that the children there and we see or hear in the same way, and that we see with the same eye, and hear with the same ear; but this is not true; that the organ is similar does not mean that the sense is."[7] Because quite a few of these children, like *Janmari*, cannot use

[7] Fernand Deligny, "Traces d'être et Bâtisse d'ombre," in *Oeuvres*, 1552.

language, there is inevitably a "wall" between them and their companions. Deligny highlights these differences between the children and the companions to such an extent that he will describe the children using terms that sound highly problematic today: at various points in his work he compares them to strange, indigenous tribes, to wild animals, to prehistoric people, and even to things. Moreover, he denies them that which belongs to the core of Binswanger's humanistic framework of thought: the "spiritual life" or the "inner core" that, according to Binswanger, is hidden in every person, whether sick or not. "(T)he ever-dangerous error is to think of the human being as a person and thus to return to the human person."[8] Deligny draws a sharp line between "beings who are conscious of being" and have a "will," and the children who, according to him, lack that consciousness and are not "wanting" in life. With this, the most fundamental contradiction between Deligny's approach and Binswanger's therapeutic practice is on the table. As we have seen, Binswanger assumes that even a severely disturbed patient exhibits a unique "life history" and a "motivational structure" that can be rebuilt with appropriate help and guidance. In doing so, he also views the mental disorder itself as a very distinct and irreplaceable "point of view" on the world and an unsuspected source of meaning and existential purpose. "The sick person (is) in a sense closer to the *Dasein* than we are—even if they are caught in a veritable dizziness of this *Dasein*." For his part, Deligny refuses to call the children in his network "subjects": they lack individuality. "Most of the children there are not *unique* if we make that word resonate with the meaning of alone, individual, distinct from others. Standing out from others is exactly what did not happen to them."[9] From the outset, Deligny points out the inability to access the internal life of these children and "communicate" with them. There is, even among autistic children who speak,

[8] Fernand Deligny, "Singulière ethnie," in *Oeuvres*, 1457.
[9] Ibid., 1387.

no real shared language, and they do not seem at first glance to be interested in the actions, let alone the thoughts and feelings, of their companions. Deligny cherishes no hope that anyone can teach them to say "I": "But sometimes when we give a sign, no sign comes back for us. Do we give a sign? It doesn't make much difference to them what we have wanted to *do* (*faire*)."[10] Consequently, when the movement maps nevertheless demonstrate a crossing between the children's wandering lines and the trajectories of their companions, this rests on nothing more than "coincidences." No true shared space is possible here ("Shared home? None of that."), no real "living together" but only a "neighbor-ing" (Deligny's neologism "*voisiner*").[11]

Perhaps Binswanger's plea for a lived understanding of the sick person's own motivations and unique points of view has brought a great deal of therapeutic benefit in recent decades. But it is certainly not the starting point for Deligny's own conceptual framework and approach. "However we try to imagine ourselves, it is impossible for us to go from our very own point of view (*point de vue*) to the way of seeing (*point de voir*) of an autistic child."[12] It is important to "realize that these are beliefs (of the child himself) and that they cannot be a starting point: whatever my ideas about what makes me happy may be, the autistic boy living nearby will not make them their own; they really don't care at all."[13] Yet this emphasis on the *otherness* of autistic youth, despite the problematic metaphors Deligny deploys for it, does not entail a dehumanizing attitude. Indeed, he makes a clear distinction between the human being/ man (*l'homme*) and the being-human (*l'humain*). This distinction is the crux of the second part of this essay. In Deligny's work, the concept of "human being" stands for the (self-)conscious, linguistic, social, communicative, and purposeful individual who is part of

---

[10] Ibid., 1387.
[11] Ibid., 1447.
[12] Deligny, "Traces d'être et Bâtisse d'ombre," 1508.
[13] Deligny, "Singulière ethnie," 1413.

civilization, and boasts that they play an important role within it. In short, his view of "human being" is identical to Binswanger's when the latter talks about the centrality of "the human being in psychiatry." But "being human," according to Deligny, indicates something quite different, and it is to this difference that he calls our attention. It is precisely the strange tribes with their enigmatic rituals and customs, the prehistoric man with their enigmatic wall drawings, the animal that stands outside human civilization, the inanimate things and, above all, the children from his "network" that show Deligny what a truly "human" existence can look like. In doing so, Deligny emphasizes that it is not *Janmari* who must adapt to his companions or his living environment; it is the companions who must "alienate" themselves in order to live in close proximity to him and the other children. "To understand, whereas the point is rather to respect the gap, and thus to alienate/become-foreign (Deligny coins the verb '*étranger*')."[14] The companions are not primarily people with their own feelings, desires, and thoughts, but a "close presence" (*présence proche*) or an "efficient vagabond" who must closely monitor the children's behaviors and movements.[15] Therefore, for these facilitators, sharpened observation is of far greater importance than confidence in a shared humanity or empathic abilities. Only through a thoroughgoing openness to these children's very own "way of being" can (the facilitators) "learn to see what does not look at them/what they have no business with ('*voir ce qui ne nous regarde pas*')."[16] With this, Deligny turns Binswanger's line of thought completely on its head. Binswanger starts from the assumption that his patients are like himself, but that they lack, in many cases only temporarily, the ability to say "I." Deligny, on the other hand, starts from the assumption that the autistic children are very different, but argues that it is primarily himself and his companions who lack something

[14] Ibid., 1472.
[15] Fernand Deligny, "Les Vagabonds efficaces," in *Oeuvres*, 161–214.
[16] Fernand Deligny, "Cahiers de l'immuable," in *Oeuvres*, 798.

fundamental. "It is we who were, 'inhibited': we could not but want."[17] And in a 1976 letter to Marxist political philosopher Louis Althusser, he writes: "What is the goal in our practice? This or that child as a 'psychotic' subject? Certainly not. The real object to be transformed is us, we there, we near these 'subjects' who are strictly speaking hardly subjects and therefore there THEY are, there."[18] Deligny therefore does not shy away from calling *Janmari* his "teacher."

But why should the autistic children in Deligny's network be in some way more "human" than their companions? We can only understand this line of thought when we come to terms with Deligny's rejection of Binswanger's existentialist framework of thought. According to Binswanger, a human being's actions and decisions acquire meaning from the awareness and acceptance of finitude and limitation: the fact that every human being will some-day die makes an individual realize that they must *decide* (and be able to justify) for themselves how they give shape to their lives. Ultimately, only death gives gravity to the projects we wish to real-ize because it is death which forces us to *choose*. Deligny, however, connects being-human to a "way of being" and "way of seeing" that are not encumbered by that awareness of finitude and limita-tion. According to him, the consciousness of finitude that belongs to the so-called human condition is absent in a boy like *Janmari*, and this precisely because he has no "consciousness of being" and is not "wanting" in life. "To this being, conceived without a shred of will, neither on his part, nor on the part of those who have nev-ertheless made him, there is nothing wanting/with him there is nothing wrong." ("À *cet être-là* ... *il ne manque rien.*")[19] Consequently, the young people in Deligny's network are not con-cerned with the question of meaning and existence. The sense of limitation and the accompanying search for a so-called "authentic" existence, so crucial to Binswanger's therapeutic approach, would

---

[17] Deligny, "Singulière ethnie," 1471.
[18] Deligny quoted in Alvarez de Toledo, "Introduction et glossaire," 1.
[19] Deligny, "Singulière ethnie," 1403.

only increase their anxieties. Therefore, according to Deligny, existential issues should not be considered a (metaphysical) foundation of a "human" life. The wandering lines of the young people in his network are not the result of a desire for meaning or a lived self. They are not records of (self-)conscious actions, decisions or choices, nor of their supposedly unconscious or "deep" drives. Strictly speaking, these lines do not express anything, not even the children's limitations or character traits. They are, according to Deligny, the opposite of an existential "project" and represent a "process of de-symbolization" and the "a-symbolic."[20] The movements that are traced in these wandering lines have taken place "for nothing" and they lack meaning and *grounding*. They point to "(a state of) *being*, not to any (metaphysical) *Being*, and tracing them does not represent anything."[21] It is precisely because these movements no longer refer to purposeful or "authentic" activities that Deligny is convinced that the young people interact with their environment in a fundamentally different way than their companions. Their randomness and seeming lack of meaning render these movements a succinct forcefulness.

Meanwhile, we understand better why Deligny puts an end to Binswanger's macabre intertwining of life and death. His frame of thinking is diametrically opposed to Binswanger's view that death contains "the necessary fulfillment of the meaning of life." The idea of an ultimate interpenetration between life and death, according to Deligny, even contributes to "humanism concealing within it fascisms, totalitarianism and all the disasters of civilization."[22] He himself refuses to call life "tragic," even when it is led by someone who has never said a single word, only rarely, and in a highly idiosyncratic way, makes contact with the outside world, and at times gets stuck moving in endless circles. Deligny counters Binswanger's emphasis on man as a *Sein-zum-Tode*, and this from the idea that life might as well be played off *against* death. He makes us consider

[20] Ibid., 1390 and 1469.
[21] Deligny, "Traces d'être et Bâtisse d'ombre," 1491 (emphasis added).
[22] Fernand Deligny, "Les détours de l'agir ou le moindre geste," in *Oeuvres*, 1249.

the possibility that, contrary to what existential psychiatry would have us believe, life may have nothing at all to do with death or impermanence. He does not understand a "human" existence from the inevitability of its *end* and, conversely, does not think of death as a "positivity" or the ground of a meaningful life. Rather, one could argue that "being human" is characterized precisely by the *ability to-not* think of death and impermanence, let alone accept them as a source of existential meaning. Being alive, for Deligny, entails that this *lack* (death, finitude, transience) is itself *lacking*. Indeed, no one has ever succeeded in truly engaging with death *from within life*, since death cannot even be adequately imagined. Life, according to Deligny, is always "shaped" in some manner, and death, in the most radical way, remains indifferent to each of our particular ambitions and projects, desires and dreams.[23] The existentialist idea that each individual must appropriate death in an "authentic" way is thus far removed from Deligny's philosophical project. For him (as for Maurice Blanchot), death is the impersonal and unformed par excellence: death does not allow itself to be readily deployed as a horizon of meaning for our highly personal choices and decisions.

Yet this emphasis on the "human" behavior of autistic children does not mean that Deligny will idealize them. In several places, he will warn that their lack of lack should not be romanticized. He realizes that it would be wrong, and inappropriate, to consider the existence of a boy like *Janmari* as "free." Nor will he attach any revolutionary or political program to it. "A libertarian (does) not in any way give in to the limitation of individual freedom (and does not recognize) that limitation, while we had to live in the presence of children for whom this vocabulary meant literally nothing and it was not in our power to awaken this desire to be free and without limits."[24] Deligny knows better than anyone else how complex the behavior of the children in his network can be, and how much they

---

[23] Ibid., 1273–1274.
[24] Deligny, "Singulière ethnie," 1431.

can disrupt the simplest actions and weekday interactions. Again and again, moreover, he emphasizes that there is a "wall" standing between the (self-)conscious, linguistic, social, communicative, and goal-oriented individual (the facilitators and himself) and the "human" children in his network. Thus, this is not an anthropological analysis or yet another definition of the human being, nor a to-be-followed example. Despite the above-mentioned description of *Janmari* as a "teacher," Deligny is not ultimately concerned with liberating himself, the companions, or us. Rather, his practice and theory are rooted in the desire to strengthen the "life raft" and "spider web" of his network from *within*. He rejects the humanist and existentialist model because it strikes him as artificial, condescending, and manipulative, unworkable for his young people. It contradicts what he sees happening around him every day and leaves unexposed an alternative but equally human way of being and seeing. And, above all, it hinders the work of care and guidance.

*   *   *

To deepen this opposition between Deligny and Binswanger, and to get a better grasp of the network that formed in the Cévennes at the end of the 1960s, we must return to the three pillars of Binswanger's *Daseinsanalysis* mentioned above. How does Deligny view the three building blocks of existential phenomenology, the concepts of world, self, and body? For Binswanger, *Ellen* counts as proof that a defective being-in-the-world, a fragmented self, and a disembodied experience of the body inevitably end up in an existential *cul-de-sac*. It is precisely because of these dysfunctions that he unabashedly calls her existence "humanly impossible" and "justifiably insane." When Deligny rejects the humanist and existentialist frame of mind, he simultaneously lays out the puzzle pieces for a very different philosophical program. A distorted being-in-the-world, a process of de-self-ing and a thing-like experience of one's own body can now no longer be dismissed as inhuman. How exactly is this argument framed?

First, Deligny opposes the premise that a human existence must be concerned with a "world," both socially and spatially. The phenomenological credo that man is oriented toward a world with others (*in-der-Welt-sein, mit-sein*) is substituted for a description of necessarily unshared experiences. The young people Deligny describes seem to be enclosed in an *idios cosmos* that cannot be aligned with a *koinos cosmos* or *koinonia*. "Who is the person who lives without the other? Well, it is *Janmari*."[25] Yet Deligny refuses to consider this social isolation as a mere negative. According to him, the therapist's task is not to "bring the patient back to earth" and thus restore a lived connection with the other: "To help them, not to love them" (*"Les aider, pas les aimer"*) becomes a first article of faith for each of his companions.[26] Deligny replaces the phenomenological notion of world with the concept of "milieu," which we can translate as a middle or between. Unlike a world, a milieu must always be *created* by the caregivers and the youth: it is never *already at hand*. With the help of well-defined actions and "gestures," every day the caretakers strive to provoke a response from the young people. The possibility of such a milieu between the caretakers and the children is determined by "tasks to be fulfilled" (*"tâches-à-faire"*). For example, Deligny describes that at times *Janmari* only manages to pass through a door with great difficulty. "If he was in a room with me and had to go out at some point, from where he was standing he could easily come up with the idea that he was too wide to go through the door. When you look at your own shoulders and you think about going through that…. Well, you can't."[27] But over time, Deligny discovers that a simple "task" can help *Janmari* get over this fear: asking him to carry an *object* into the other room suddenly gets him through the door. The "tasks" that can create a milieu in this way are related to activities that at first glance appear to be insignificant. Thus in *Ce gamin, là* we see how the attendants

---

[25] Fernand Deligny, "Le Croire et le Craindre," in *Oeuvres*, 1198. See also idem, "Les Détours de l'agir," 1251–1253.

[26] Deligny, "Les Vagabonds efficaces," 207.

[27] Deligny, "Le Croire et le Craindre," 1091.

indiscriminately hit a barrel or piece of wood with a stick and after a while the youngsters start doing something similar. And we already mentioned the scenes in which the youths knead dough, side by side with companions who are doing the same thing. Deligny does not view these activities as meaningful, shared activities or collaborations with the companions. He situates them in a forever-to-be-constructed between, and not in a once-and-for-all retrieved world. They do not, in his view, presuppose a recovered awareness of an external, shared space. For the task of acting purposefully in a shared world would cause unrest or anxiety in these young people, because it would be accompanied by social pressure and a whole series of unexpected events. When certain "gestures" of the facilitators elicit a response from the youths, their actions may run parallel, but they are not anchored in a social world, according to Deligny. This thought, too, marks a point of difference from Binswanger, who, while mindful of people's "gestures," understands them as a meaningful externalization of a person and their "soulful life."[28] Deligny is not concerned with the lived attunement between the experiential worlds and intentions of individuals but with different "rhythms" that "intersect" for a moment at most. Consequently, Deligny sees an almost unbridgeable distance between the making (*faire*) of the facilitators and the doing (*agir*) of the young people. A making process is purposeful and concerned with an external world, while the doing of these young people seems to be a mere means without a proper end. When one of the youths, Anne, repeatedly plunges stones in a bottle of water, this is unrelated to the wish "that the stones would be clean." That would be but an "interpretation contaminated with the obedience to the *to*, indispensable for us to understand or allow something."[29] Anne's doing has nothing to do with such instrumental considerations and rational actions. It primarily illustrates an ability to "respond" to certain, seemingly insignificant objects, materials, or events. When *Janmari* kneads

---

[28] Ludwig Binswanger, "Erfahren, Verstehen, Deuten in der Psychoanalyse," in *Ausgewählte Werke. Band 3. Vorträge und Aufsätze*, 5.

[29] Deligny, "Les Détours de l'agir," 1252.

dough in *Ce gamin, là* we will thus need to understand the eventual baking of bread at most as a consequence and not as the goal of his actions. Decisive here is a fascination for certain gestures and textures, provoked by the companions.[30]

Deligny's aversion to a phenomenological interpretation of the notion of "shared world" is further evidenced by a second argument: the gesture is an interruption and not a discovery or creation of meanings. For authors such as Husserl, Heidegger, and thus also Binswanger, the notion of world stands for a unit of meaning and experience. According to them, the orientation toward a shared world ensures that disparate things and experiences can be related to one another within a single overarching whole. Conversely, according to them, the disintegration of that whole of relations, meanings, and references will cause certain objects and experiences to become disconcertingly autonomous and throw the individual back upon themselves. In other words, within a phenomenological framework, the fragmentation of the world inevitably runs into anxiety and despair. But Deligny sees exactly the opposite happening with the young people in his network. For them, the many possible links between different objects and experiences are a source of anxiety and disorientation. The sense that each thing can be placed in a chain of relationships and meanings with other things is extremely confusing to them. Therefore, these young people look for a particular detail, object, or phenomenon that isolates itself somewhat from the rest. A drop of water, a ball of clay, a wooden block in a stone basin, a broom, or, even more simply, the movement of an eyelash elicit the interest of these young people precisely because they seem to exist on their own and no longer refer to anything else. It is for this reason that Deligny urges the companions to organize a "way out" (*détour*) of meaning by making their gestures appear "intentionless." In this way, they seem to have taken place "for nothing." He describes this "surplus" or "remainder" with the word "*orné.*" The gestures of the companions give the impression of being "too much" or merely ornamental and of

---

[30] Ibid., 1291.

having no functional value. Only on this condition can they result in a momentary but welcome interruption of an overarching unity of meaning and experience. According to Deligny, then, gestures have nothing to do with language, not even with a language-without-words. "While I see human space as littered with 'intersections,' others see it as populated with symbols, and it is clear that 'intersections' and symbols do not go well together."[31] The children seem to be primarily in search of a creative being-*out*-of-the-world that, somewhat paradoxically, feeds off the tangible reality of a milieu. Thus, the opening up of the world is here not a matter of fantasy but of a physical response to concrete gestures, actions, and things. It is these "points of reference" (*repères*) that for a moment create the possibility of a productive escape from the constraints of language and shared meanings. "*Janmari* does not recognize *me*, that *me* is anybody. But when there is a *something*, *Janmari*'s attentiveness is complete."[32] Thanks to the establishment of a milieu, gestures, actions, and things are disconnected from the network of rational or symbolic meanings, linguistic references, and "worldly" relations. This, in Deligny's view, suffices to uncouple the young from their endless routines and automatisms for a while.

The philosophers Gilles Deleuze and Félix Guattari would later use this conceptual framework, and Deligny's notion of wandering line, as inspiration for their own concept of "*ligne de fuite*," or line of flight. In their view, the maps of Deligny and his colleagues provide evidence for the "rhizomatic nature" of human desire.[33] Deleuze and Guattari decouple human desire from Oedipal schemas and the so-called spontaneous fixation on the mother and father figure with which Freudian psychoanalysis associates infantile sexuality. When our understanding of human desire is enclosed in such rigid schemas it loses its inherently productive capacity and is

---

[31] Ibid., 1253.

[32] Deligny, "Traces d'être et Bâtisse d'ombre," 1499.

[33] Gilles Deleuze and Félix Guarrari, *A Thousand Plateaus. Capitalism and Schizophrenia*, transl. Brian Massumi (Minneapolis: University of Minnesota Press, 1987), 11–14.

characterized by an inevitable deficit or lack. Indeed, the supposedly first object of desire is declared inaccessible by the prohibition of incest, which would make it clash with all sorts of taboos and coercive restrictions from the very beginning. Even if Deligny shuns the use of the word desire, it is partly his frame of mind that inspires Deleuze and Guattari in their fundamental rethinking and recalibration of Freudian psychoanalysis. For them, there are no natural or biological laws that determine the human drive and lead us to desire only a certain set of, and always the same, individuals, actions, or objects. The libido is above all "world-historical":[34] it obtains its energy and activity from a concrete and tangible milieu of discoverable phenomena and properties. Within that complex network, there is no guiding or structuring role for the mother or father figure, nor for the underlying personality traits or identity of the desiring individual. "A milieu is made up of qualities, substances, powers, and events: the street, for example, with its materials (paving stones), its noises (the cries of merchants), its animals (harnessed horses) or its dramas (a horse slips, a horse falls down, a horse is beaten ...). ... Nothing is more instructive than the paths of autistic children, such as those whose maps Deligny has revealed and superimposed, with their customary lines, wandering lines, loops, corrections, and turnings back—all their singularities."[35] The many "lines" that connect an individual to the phenomena and qualities of their living environment are fundamentally open to change and renewal. They are charged with an intensity that defies prohibitions or taboos. It is from these unexpected encounters with their "milieu" that human desire is ignited and can develop into a force of renewal. This is why Deleuze and Guattari do away with the *interpretive* character of psychoanalysis: they are not concerned with uncovering the hidden, unconscious, or repressed meanings that encumber an individual's well-being but with pointing out and

---

[34] Gilles Deleuze, 'What Children Say', in *Essays Critical and Clinical*, transl. Daniel W. Smith and Michael A. Greco (Minneapolis: University of Minnesota Press, 1997), 62.

[35] Ibid., 61.

stimulating particular rhythms that can lead an individual to pro-
duce themselves anew. They highlight that Deligny's maps have no
archaeological-genealogical function and do not refer to the "profound link between the unconscious and memory." The search for
defining "origins" is here exchanged for an effectuation of productive "*displacements*": "Every map is a redistribution of impasses and
breakthroughs, of thresholds and enclosures, which necessarily go
from bottom to top. There is not only a reversal of directions, but
also a difference in nature: the unconscious no longer deals with
persons and objects, but with trajectories and becomings; it is no
longer an unconscious of commemoration but one of mobilization,
an unconscious whose objects take flight rather than remaining
buried in the ground."[36]

Deleuze and Guattari will associate Deligny's project with a particular form of (micro)politics. Since there is no guiding or structuring role for the authority of, say, parents or society, human desire
is endowed with a force of resistance and even community building.
It is also from this force that a form of social change can be conceived. "It is certain that [Deligny's lines of flight] have nothing to
do with a structure, which is never occupied by anything more than
points and positions, by arborescences, and which always forms a
closed system, precisely in order to prevent escape. Deligny invokes
a common Body upon which these lines are inscribed as so many
segments, thresholds, or quanta, territorialities, deterritorializa-
tions, or reterritorializations."[37] On the other hand, Deligny's
framework helps Deleuze and Guattari come to terms with the
inseparability of the experience of our immediate environment and
our imagination. The trajectories marked on Deligny's maps are
more than a reproduction of bodily movements. They indicate at
which moments, in which places, with which objects, and in
response to which events the encounter with tangible reality gives
rise to an undeniable sense of non-exhausted possibility. This

---

[36] Ibid., 63.
[37] Deleuze and Guarrari, *A Thousand Plateaus*, 203.

feeling is not merely illusory because it indicates a real capacity, a force of human desire. For Deleuze, this is a "vision" in which images that have no reality value in themselves are, as it were, *added to* the experience of that reality, injecting it with a special tension. Deleuze thereby starts from the fact that reality, in its mere existence, is quite powerless: it "lacks the force necessary to be reflected in the imagination."[38] The imagination, in itself, is no less weak: "by itself, (it) does not have the force ... to be verified in the real."[39] Deligny's maps demonstrate for Deleuze the special intensity that comes from the *blending together* of reality and image, however different the two may be: "This is why the imaginary and the real must be, rather, like two juxtaposable or superimposable parts of a single trajectory, two faces that ceaselessly interchange with one another, a mobile mirror."[40]

Deligny's faith in the possibility of a creative being-out-of-the-world sheds light on his experiments with film. As early as the 1950s, while still affiliated to the "alternative" psychiatric institution La Grande Cordée, he deploys the film camera as an "educational tool." He gives autistic adolescents the task of recording each other and their surroundings on film. Deligny introduces the neologism *camérer* as an alternative to the word *filmer* because the final product, the final film, no longer matters here. He bets on an "intentionless" use of the camera. This free use of the camera could reveal gestures and points of reference that would otherwise remain undiscovered. However, camérer has nothing to do with the desire for an accurate representation of the world. Deligny assigns the camera a similar task as the movement maps, but now it is the children who are in control, thereby creating the conditions for a radically *new* interaction with their environment. Again, Deligny stresses the possibility of a creative *way out* of meaning. Camérer "would mean respecting that which is meaningless, says nothing, does not address us, in other words escapes the symbolic

---

[38] Deleuze, 'What Children Say,' 62.

[39] Ibid., 62–63.

[40] Ibid. 63.

domestication without which there would be no history, for lack of consciousness, individual or collective."[41] Thus, the camera is neither world-building nor meaning-giving: it does not give a human face or *Stimmung* to particular things or phenomena and does not establish a new overarching context of meaning. Deligny's experiments with film are at odds with the search for the supposedly mysterious beauty of the everyday or the undiscovered poetry or expressiveness of the banal. On the contrary, as a nonhuman, mechanical eye, the camera helps to disconnect mundane details, objects, or experiences from the many references attached to them in everyday life. The camera exposes the special power of the *expressionless* and isolates an object or human being in its mechanical reproduction. Thus, it suspends for a moment the search for shared meaning and restores in the young people a confidence in the possibility of renewal and metamorphosis. According to Deligny, the non-worldly and expressionless space of the film image gives these young people new "reasons to be."[42] "Camérer, that would mean grabbing them, the images, because you never know, because we will see." Deligny focuses on "exploiting a small grinding space that makes us go in a different direction from the course of history, from events being what they are, and being lived by people, though 'being lived' is a lot to say."[43] The camera enables the young people to *fashion* the world *anew*, as a milieu to which they can *respond*. For them, it provides proof that a living environment can become *different*.

But in the end, of course, Deligny is not so much concerned with the living environment of these young people but, above all, with those young people themselves. The descriptions of a creative being-out-of-the-world bring us to his interpretation of the

---

[41] Fernand Deligny, "Camérer," in *Oeuvres*, 1744. See also Johanna Cockx, 'Le moindre geste (1962–1971). An entry into the cinema and the thought of Fernand Deligny' (2022), see https://www.sabzian.be/text/le-moindre-geste-1962-1971.

[42] Fernand Deligny, "La caméra outil pédagogique," in *Oeuvres*, 417.

[43] Deligny, "Camérer," 1745.

concept of "self." In *Ce gamin, là,* we had already heard him say that the "famous SELF" in *Janmari is* "in fact/absent/empty," that he "revolves around NOTHING" nor is he "looking for himself." The absence of a coherent identity or a stable self is not necessarily symptomatic of a "humanly impossible" existence, as Binswanger would have it. On the contrary, according to Deligny, "being-human" entails what we might call a process of de-self-ing. As a young boy, he was already fascinated by the possibility that our self uncouples from itself at crucial moments and thus copes with unexpected problems and obstacles. For example, Deligny describes how as a three-and-a-half-year-old toddler, during World War I, he did not dare to walk through the school gates. The story reads like an echo of the anecdote with *Janmari* but here Deligny explains that entering was accompanied by an internal separation of the self: "Certainly, I entered, but something remained outside; the subject entered: the good subject, or the naughty subject, depending on the moment. The subject went back to school, as it should, because it had to, but something remained outside, something very vital, some weed."[44] I and self are always at most provisional for Deligny, and this realization, too, spills over into a sense of as yet unrealized possibilities. This experience that a particular identity might as well be abandoned has remained decisive for him throughout his life. In 1955, for example, he meets Maurice A., a seventeen-year-old boy with a severe addiction to alcohol. Deligny puts him to work in a small shipyard where he can work with plaster and cement. All this he captures on pellicle. The film footage is not a record of a stable or rooted self, because it is at odds with the real situation of Maurice who is by no means freed from his alcohol addiction: "The enemy, for him, is the bar. The enemy is numerous." Yet according to Deligny, these to some extent false images provide tangible proof that Maurice will be able to be helped. For precisely because they cut the link with the real Maurice, these images carry the promise of a *new* and *different* Maurice. "If what I believe is true, that new intentions change one's perception of the world, then Maurice A.,

---

[44] Deligny, "Le Croire et le Craindre," 1092.

with his future company in mind, is no longer on the same earth as Maurice A., a precocious construction worker, who learned to drink by comrades who wanted to do nothing wrong by treating him as an equal, by handing him the bottle when they themselves were drinking."[45] According to Deligny, then, it is not only a cliché but an outright misconception that the young people in his network would be locked into "themselves." By responding to all kinds of "references" in their environment, the very possibility of another self becomes tangible to them. Their "doing," frees them from the compulsion to say "I" all the time and neutralizes the demand for a stable and socially acceptable identity.

In this regard as well Deligny completely reverses Binswanger's manner of reasoning. For Binswanger, the human being is an individual among other individuals: each person is marked by their own life history but can learn to relate to other individuals by virtue of a similarity to them. In that process, identification, empathy, and living-together play a crucial role: the self can push its boundaries and extend its reach to the point where it can feel itself *in* or *with* someone else, as it were. Deligny, however, connects being-human not to a unique and "undivided" flow of life but to a *shared capacity*. What characterizes autistic adolescents is not that they have over the years built up a very distinct and continuous internal life but that they repeatedly find the power to interrupt an external context of meaning. Being-human, according to Deligny, lies in that ability to respond to the situations described above. Those reactions exemplify, on the one hand, an openness to certain things and phenomena *in* the external world and, on the other hand, the ability to bring to life a line of flight *from* the world, building from just that openness. Moreover, these wandering lines or lines of flight are a corporeal reaction to what is doomed to remain "strange," what is "meaningless, saying nothing." They thus have nothing to do with recognizing a resemblance to others, nor with identification, empathy, or living-together. In other words, Deligny's notion of

---

[45] Deligny, "La caméra outil pédagogique," 417.

being-human revolves around feeling-*out* rather than feeling-*in* (*em*-pathy) or feeling-with (*sym*-pathy). Here, a process of de-selfing breaks squarely through the boundaries of the I rather than merely extending those boundaries and thus even further expanding the reach of the self.

Let us develop this line of thought a little further from the perspective of its opposition to Binswanger's phenomenological framework. In his case study of *Ellen*, Binswanger describes repetition as an obstacle to a healthy personal development: it is symptomatic of an addict's insatiable urge to "stop time," to be dominated by the past, and to bog himself down in an "empty" present. Deligny, however, sees precisely repetition as central to the youth's responsive capacities. When they respond to the gestures of the facilitators or to certain objects and phenomena in their environment, it happens primarily in the form of repetition: just like the facilitators, the young people hit a barrel or wooden block with a stick, knead dough, go to work with a broom, etc. So, surprisingly, it is thanks to a certain form of repetition that these youths are able to overcome their compulsive behavior. Such a form of repetitive behavior has nothing more to do with the compulsive staying in circles and moving back and forth of *Ellen* and *Janmari*. In fact, it is their opposite. As a condition for the young people's responding or "doing," repetitiveness is for Deligny eminently active: "Repetition, like tracing, exists as an infinitive, it is a form of doing. ... Doing is always an initiative even if it seems to us to be merely repetitive."[46] These "active" repetitions have nothing to do with patterns of identification, the imitation of a model or the "as if" that underpins processes of symbolization. They do not even have an interindividual or socializing function: they do not build identity but break it open. According to Deligny, then, this form of repetition is primarily related to a particular relationship to *things* or *natural phenomena*. For example, he refers to an incident during the summer of 1968 in which *Janmari* starts banging his head uncontrollably

---

[46] Deligny, "Traces d'être et Bâtisse d'ombre," 1552.

against the wall at two in the morning. Nothing or no one could calm him down. Until one of the companions takes him outside and he catches sight of a stone that had been wrenched loose from a wall the morning before to clamp down on a wooden structure: "*Janmari* storms over to it, pulls the stone out from under it and puts it back into the wall. Return, gone dismay: sleep."[47] The children seem to feel somehow supported by the specific way of being of things and natural elements. Objects and natural phenomena also lack the "consciousness of being" and the "will" and the supposed connection between life and the *end* of life is cut: although they can be broken or destroyed, they cannot *die* and they have no awareness of *mortality*. That is why they play a role in the process of de-self-ing which, contrary to what Binswanger has to say about it, Deligny believes is of great therapeutic importance. Here, too, the camera has a special role to play. Deligny sees a natural connection between the camera and *les choses* (things) because they also "have no history." Things do not set up an internal, unique, and unbroken stream of life over time and their existence is not lived out in light of a *purpose*. For this reason, he dreams of being able to capture on pellicule the endlessly slow, and seemingly pointless, process of a melting iceberg: "(H)ow much time that takes, this mass of which nothing will remain but an ice cube, first the size of a fist, then nothing at all; nothing more than the sea."[48] The camera captures the disappearance of the ice block, but there is no dying or death involved, not even a real ending. The attentiveness to this very specific, ahistorical life of certain objects and natural phenomena also spills over into a heightened sensitivity to metamorphosis and change. "Becoming water seems to (these young people) more tempting than becoming like us."[49] Deligny also attributes to the young a specific "memory of the species" that is drawn to the remnants of lost and broken objects. These young people may be "without history," but they are by no means without a past. Five or

---

[47] Deligny, "Singulière ethnie," 1472.
[48] Deligny, "Camérer," 1743.
[49] Ibid., 1745.

six years after an earthen ashtray broke, *Janmari* suddenly arrives with its debris, as if it is only there that real life can be found for him. "*Janmari* stood in the open doorway; a turn, and he was gone, down the stairs. What he brought back ten minutes later, in the hollow of a careful hand, was a small mound of mud, a mixture of earth and wet ash. ... In the mud were the shards of a clay pot that had served as an ashtray many years before and had stood there constantly."[50] Roads that have long since decayed also arouse a distinct fascination in these young people, as if they never quite disappeared for them. It is almost as if, in these forgotten and lost elements, the young people recover a life, or rather a sur-vival (literally: "over-life") that death has shaken off.

Deligny links this repetition of the sur-vival of things and natural phenomena to a specific experience of the human body. He too distinguishes a "lived" or "existential" and a "mechanical" or disembodied experience of the body (*Leib* and *Körper*, respectively). In his view, however, the autistic adolescents prove that precisely this disembodied experience of one's own body can force a therapeutic breakthrough. When the fascination with the independent life of a particular object or element of nature frees the youngsters for a moment from their compulsive behavior, this is accompanied by the experience that their own bodies, too, seem essentially alien to them. With *Janmari*, for example, "the hands seem to lack the sense of 'belonging.' (That sense of belonging is) self-evident to us—or comes from that self."[51] When the young people in the network respond to their environment, they have themselves almost become a "thing among things." In those cases the spontaneous identification with a "lived" and "proper" body is missing: "(I)t is true that an autistic person is attached to these things scattered across the field of reference, while he is not attached to his hands, or rather, everything happens as if those hands were not attached to

[50] Deligny, "Singulière ethnie," 1454. See also Perret, "Le tacite, l'humain," 307–352.
[51] Deligny, "Les Détours d'agir," 1290.

him, which is to say that they do not belong to him."[52] This "thing-like" and disembodied physicality is the direct opposite of the "wearing out," "becoming a doll," and "merely vegetating" that Binswanger associates with such a state. It has nothing to do with the "non-form" (*Ungestalt*) that he believes can only be "*lived out*." In several places in his work, Deligny refers to clowns, acro-bats, circuses, and slapstick as proof that the apparent reduction of the human body to an inanimate object can give a "stylish," "danc-ing," and vital impression: "it's burlesque, it's funny, it's human."[53] The mechanical and disembodied *Körper* may seem devoid of all *agency* but it is not passive. When even one's own body is experi-enced as a thing among things, it actually increases one's attention to possible points of connection in one's surroundings. With *Janmari*, "the state of alertness does not extend to these omitted hands, (which are) like a temporarily omitted tool, while this alert-ness does remain intact with respect to sounds, even in the distance, and surrounding things."[54] A disembodied experience of the body can bring these young people into proximity with the self-contained form and sur-vival of things and nature.

With his descriptions of the behavior of these autistic children, Deligny wants us to think the unthinkable: these young people, who, according to him, are not concerned with meaning, language, or symbolization and remain indifferent to the search for a ground for their existence, seem at times to have *become* the very ground of their existence. Their idiosyncratic interactions with certain things and elements of nature express a capacity to break down their envi-ronment into precisely those fragments that matter to them, and only to them. In these moments, they manage to reopen the world, as it were, according to their own idée-fixes and focal points, how-ever strange these may be to everyone else. In a similar context, Binswanger speaks of the "inconsequence of natural experience,"

---

[52] Ibid., 1290.

[53] Ibid., 1309. For one of many references to dance, see Fernand Deligny, "Nous et l'innocent," in *Oeuvres*, 785.

[54] Deligny, "Les Détours d'agir," 1290.

namely, the inability to let things be as they are.[55] This inability, he says, is an essential characteristic of schizophrenia, and he sees it as purely negative. The patient is deemed incapable of accepting the fact that reality does not conform to their ideal image and believed to strive to undo this structural gap. As we have seen, this gap between reality and the ideal takes on enormous proportions for *Ellen* and she becomes trapped in the desire to "want to escape her fate." Deligny, however, describes this inconsequence, and the inability to recognize reality as it is, as one of the basic characteristics of human behavior among the young people in his network. Without losing sight of the fact that the "doing" of these autistic children is independent of will and intention, and without romanticizing it as an example of total freedom, Deligny discovers in their behavior the power to become, indeed, the creator of one's own destiny. These children do seem capable of meeting the world entirely on their own terms. It is for this reason that Deligny no longer interprets the companions' task as the search for a focused alignment with the external world "as it is" but as the "creation of circumstances." In their actions, the world is constantly rejuvenated as something "other." In this way, the facilitators ensure that precisely the non-intentional and unexpected can become a familiar presence for these young people.[56] Their lines of flight and wandering lines then do not merely bring about a *"refuge"*: they ensure that what is most inhibiting and confusing for these young people largely gives way to a universe in which they *can* function. Through a particular way of acting and reacting, an environment is created on a daily basis that does present the young people with a sense of coherence and unity, although it cannot be shared with others.

[55] See Ludwig Binswanger, "Einleitung: Schizophrenia," in *Ausgewählte Werke. Band 4. Der Mensch in der Psychiatrie*, 335–337.

[56] See also Perret, "Le tacite, l'humain," 111–165.

CHAPTER 4

Coda

Abstract The "Coda" further explores the theoretical confrontation between psychiatrists Binswanger and Deligny. It delves into the potential alternate history had Binswanger adopted Deligny's approach in his institution. The document critically examines the voices that narrate *Ellen*'s story, most of which are male and heavily mediated. It also highlights the paradoxical interweaving of life and death in *Ellen*'s case. The document further discusses the case of Aby Warburg, an art scholar and cultural anthropologist, who, unlike *Ellen*, was able to recover after a stay at Bellevue. The coda concludes by exploring Warburg's belief in the therapeutic power of his own thinking and the similarities to Deligny's project.

Keywords Aby Warburg • Fragment • Art • Symbol • Attentiveness

I have already mentioned it before: the purely theoretical confrontation between Binswanger and Deligny involves the search for an *alternate history*. No one will ever know what would have happened had Binswanger organized his institution in Kreuzlingen like Deligny's network in the Cévennes. How would *Ellen*, scion of a

© The Author(s), under exclusive license to Springer Nature   59
Switzerland AG 2024
S. Symons, *Ludwig Binswanger and Fernand Deligny on the Human Condition*, https://doi.org/10.1007/978-3-031-66123-5_4

wealthy and aristocratic family, have reacted to being asked to participate in everyday household and kitchen tasks as baking bread, washing dishes, and sweeping the floor? Could these daily concerns have provided an unexpected wealth of gestures and points of "reference" for her as well? Or would they have further increased the male domination that *Ellen* had been subjected to all along?[1] Essentially, these are pointless questions. Very little is known about the day-to-day organization at Binswanger's institution and the actual practices that were deployed there. Moreover, *Ellen*'s case study consists of a variety of (male) authorial voices that are woven together in a complex, and constructed, narrative. All too often, these voices claim to speak in *Ellen*'s name, while her words have in truth been drastically mediated and modified through editorial interventions. Binswanger did not read his patient's diaries until after her death and all of the material that he based his case-study on was either written or compiled by *Ellen*'s husband, *Karl*. Consequently, there is no hope of gaining a direct access to the most profound and personal layers of *Ellen*'s mind.[2] However, it is striking that the many references to an insatiable zest for life in *Ellen*'s diaries completely eluded Binswanger. In several places, she speaks of an "unsatisfied drive" and "unbridled ambition" that contradict the *Todgeweihtheit* her therapist attributes to her: "It boils and throbs inside me, as if something inside me wants to break through its shell! Freedom! Revolution!"[3] Similarly, her descriptions of animals (horses and worms, among others) and elements of nature (the earth, fields, and mountains, among others) could have shed a very different light on her idée-fixes and obsessions. Who knows, maybe they could have been a starting point for the construction of a milieu, a "life raft," a "spider web." It was not to be.

---

[1] For an excellent overview of feminist readings of the *Ellen*-case and highly relevant archival work, see Naamah Akavia, "Writing 'The Case of Ellen West': Clinical Knowledge and Historical Representation," *Science in Context* 21 (1) (2008), 119–144.

[2] Ibid.

[3] *Ellen*, quoted in Binswanger, *Ellen West*, 24.

Yet at times history shows itself from an unexpectedly generous side. Then it seems as if an unrealized possibility has nestled itself in the lap of verified events. As if an *alternate* history has rubbed up against the course of *actual* history and even become entangled with it. At such moments, the course of events abruptly takes a very different turn than expected. What seemed a mere possibility finally becomes, undeniably, a reality. That, at least, is the impression I get when reading the story of the patient brought to Bellevue on April 16, 1921, less than three weeks after *Ellen* left the institution. The 54-year-old man, too, comes from a wealthy and powerful family. Coincidentally, he is even related to *Ellen*. Unlike *Ellen* and *Janmari*, we do know this man by name. He is Aby Warburg (1866–1929), one of the most renowned art scholars and cultural anthropologists of the twentieth century.[4] Like *Ellen*, he is in particularly bad shape when he arrives in Kreuzlingen. Ever since the outbreak of World War I, he has struggled with horrific, blood-soaked hallucinations, haunting delusions, and severe depression. In the months before his arrival, he stayed in an institution in Jena, Germany, where at one point he tried to strangle a nurse and became convinced that they were serving him the flesh of his own children as a meal. The director of this institution, Hans Berger, preferred to get rid of him because his loud screams disturbed the peace of the other patients. Upon his arrival in Kreuzlingen, Warburg is firmly convinced that he is being taken to prison and that his relatives are being tortured there. He defends himself in every possible way against that manifest injustice. During the first conversations with Binswanger, Warburg hurls insults and calls him a "demon," "a swine," a "vulture." The director of Bellevue remains calm under the circumstances. At first he diagnoses his new patient as schizophrenic, until Kraepelin convinces him that this is manic-depression. No mention of the recently introduced term "autism"

---

[4] For an extensive discussion of Warburg's illness history, his stay in Bellevue, and his relationship with Binswanger, see Ludwig Binswanger-Aby Warburg, *Die unendliche Heilung. Aby Warburg's Krankengeschichte*, ed. Chantal Marazia and Davide Stimilli (Berlin: Diaphanes, 2007).

is made anywhere but that he is at times severely psychotic is beyond dispute. Once again the same miserable refrain we heard with *Ellen* and *Janmari* resounds: Warburg is "incurable." To Freud, Binswanger confides that he "does not believe that a recovery from the condition before acute psychosis and a return to research activities are possible."[5]

Still.

Warburg will indeed be declared cured after a stay of nearly three years and a half at Bellevue and will be able to leave for home. On August 12, 1924, he will be discharged from the institution and travel to Hamburg, in the company of Binswanger and two nurses. A year later, contrary to his own earlier statements, Binswanger will proclaim that his former patient can be "released as normal" once and for all.[6] Indeed, until his death in 1929, Warburg leads a fairly stable life in the new building he has had constructed for his gigantic and legendary research library.

*   *   *

How could this happy ending, so different from *Ellen's*, be explained? First, it is striking that Warburg seizes every moment of mental stability during his stay at Bellevue to continue working on his art-historical and cultural-anthropological research project. Indeed, he firmly believes that his "scientific practice" is his "only cure." For this reason, he continues to read and write as much as he can about the themes that have inspired him throughout his life. Thus it happens that Warburg discovers in his own thinking the "points of reference" that Deligny will later describe so meticulously for us. For Warburg, it is certain that only a "return to his

---

[5] See Sigmund Freud and Ludwig Binswanger, *Briefwechsel, 1908–1938*, ed. Gerhard Fichtner (Frankfurt: Fischer, 1992), 176. See also Peter Loewenberg, "Aby Warburg, the Hopi Serpent Ritual and Ludwig Binswanger," *Psychoanalysis and History* 19, 1 (2017), 88.

[6] Binswanger in a letter to Warburg dated August 14, 1925, in *Die unendliche Heilung*, 141.

professional research" will prove that he can "save himself from this chaos."[7] Understanding the supposed therapeutic qualities of Warburg's scholarly activities involves, first of all, coming to terms with what can be called the "elective affinities" between his life and work. In an autobiographical fragment from September 1922, Warburg mentions the fever phantasies that have troubled him from the age of six onward. These hallucinations come with "fear" [*Furcht*] and "disproportioned contextless image-memories."[8] The scholarly tools and strategies that enable Warburg to analyze Western culture undoubtedly facilitate a better grasp of these mental agonies. His art historical work builds on the observation that deep-seated forces of disharmony and unrest are similarly ingrained within the heart of Western civilization at large. *Pace* the influential Renaissance scholar Winckelmann, who held that the renewed interest in Greek and Roman antiquity underlying Western modernity was tantamount to a recovery of logos and stability, Warburg insists that it was in truth a response to and an illustration of entrenched and collective anxieties.[9] To describe this irrational undercurrent of the Western Renaissance Warburg takes recourse to philosophical, historical, and art-theoretical concepts that uncannily mirror his own mental symptoms.[10] His own unique strand of

[7] See, among others, the following passages in letters and diary entries by Warburg, in *Die unendliche Heilung*, 100, 101, 102, 105, 108, 111, and 114.

[8] Warburg, 'Erstes autobiographisches Fragment', in ibidem., 101.

[9] For a clear summary of Warburg's most important art-historical ideas, see the work of Matthew Rampley, e.g., 'Iconology of the Interval: Aby Warburg's Legacy', *Word & Image: A Journal of Verbal/Visual Enquiry* 17, 4 (2001): 303–324 and 'From Symbol to Allegory: Aby Warburg's Theory of Art', in *The Art Bulletin* 79, 1 (1997): 41–55.

[10] Georges Didi-Huberman's path-breaking study on Warburg is the prime source to understand the parallels between Warburg's art-historical method and his mental condition. See his *The Survival of Images. Phantoms of Time and Time of Phantoms. Aby Warburg's History of Art*, transl. Harvey L. Menselsohn (University Park, Pennsylvania: The Pennsylvania State University Press, 2017), esp. Chapter 2.

iconology is built on what he calls a "psycho-history" of art. This is, for instance, how he describes his life/work at Kreuzlingen. "Sometimes it looks to me as if, in my role as a psycho-historian, I tried to diagnose the schizophrenia of Western civilization from its images in an autobiographical reflex. The ecstatic 'Nympha' (manic) on the one side and the mourning river-god (depressive) on the other."[11] Warburg's attention goes out to "symptomatic forces" that charge otherwise still images with heterogeneous and impure temporalities.[12] Warburg not only adopts (and adapts) the Nietzschean couple of Apollonian and Dionysian forces but also takes recourse to an explicitly *clinical* vocabulary that at times appears to have been lifted straight from the pages of his medical reports.

When one looks at the *content* of Warburg's professional research, some similarities to Deligny's project are unmistakable. During the first decades of the twentieth century, Warburg also works on a conceptual framework that can count as an alternative to the phenomenology and existentialism that take shape in those same years. Warburg knew not only Binswanger but also Husserl personally (Husserl visited him in Bellevue on August 15, 1923) but would himself take a very different direction.[13] As an art historian and cultural anthropologist, Warburg's background is, of course, not that of Deligny. Nevertheless, he too will point out to us the specific

[11] Aby Warburg, Journal, April 3, 1929, quoted in Ernst Gombrich, *Aby Warburg. An Intellectual Biography* (London: The Warburg Institute, University of London, 1970), 303.

[12] For but one reference to the "symptomatic significance" of artistic motifs, see Warburg, 'Francesco Sassetti's Last Injunctions to His Sons', in Aby Warburg, *The Renewal of Pagan Antiquity*, intr. Kurt W. Forster, transl. David Britt (Los Angeles: The Getty Research Institute for the History of Arts and the Humanities, 1999), 249.

[13] For an account of Husserl's visit to Bellevue, see Thomas Vongehr, 'Aus dem Schatzkästlein des Husserl-Archivs: Am Bodensee 1923. Husserl und die Psychiatrie. Husserl trifft Ludwig Binswanger und Aby Warburg,' *Husserl Archiv Mitteilungsblatt* 33 (2010), 11–16.

nature of certain details and objects that detach themselves from an overarching context of meaning and thus prepare a creative line of escape from the world. Like Deligny, he calls these details "gestures," and he wants to study them in an "art history without text."[14] From 1905 onward, Warburg describes these motifs as *Pathosformeln*, that is, expressive formulas of affects and energies that are at least partly derived from an inherited, pagan, and highly dynamic repertoire of Greek, Roman, and Eastern elements. With this concept he calls attention to the very specific, non-discursive life-force of certain things and natural phenomena. He discovers these gestures and pathos formulas especially in the paintings and frescoes of early Renaissance masters such as Domenico Ghirlandaio and Sandro Botticelli. Warburg's best-known examples are folds in clothing, hair blowing in the wind, and dancing nymphs: as heterogeneous elements, they break the unity of meaning and figural

[14] The most notorious reference to the "intensification of outward movement" (*Darstellung äußerlich bewegten Beiwerks*) can be found in the "Prefatory Note" to Warburg's "Sandro Botticelli's *Birth of Venus* and *Spring*. An Examination of Concepts of Antiquity in the Italian Renaissance" (1893), in *The Renewal of Pagan Antiquity*, 89. See also the reference to "the surface mobility of inanimate accessory forms, draperies and hair" and the description of "the most difficult problem in all art" as "that of capturing images of life in motion," in ibidem., 141; and Aby Warburg, 'Der Eintritt des antikisierenden Idealstils in die Malerei der Frührenaissance. – Florenz, Kunsthistorisches Institut 20. IV. 914' in *Werke*, red. Martin Treml, Sigrid Weigel and Perdita Ladwig, with Susanne Hetzer, Herbert Kopp-Oberstebrink and Christina Oberstebrink (Frankfurt-am-Main: Suhrkamp, 2018), 281.

tranquility with which early Renaissance art is usually associated.[15] For Warburg, these, indeed, wandering lines will remain a particularly vitalizing feature. They strengthen him in the conviction that the intensity of an image can never be pinned down to shared and inherited, linguistic references. Rather, these motifs of movement represent the survival, or in his words "after-life" of pagan motifs from antiquity. Millennia after that period ended, Dionysian, irrational impulses emerge in the folds of a cloak, the waving of hair, or the theme of the dancing nymph, disrupting the calmness of humanist anthropocentrism. Like the "disproportioned contextless image-memories" he refers to in his personal diary, Warburg believes that these motifs somehow exceed the grasp of rational understanding. *Pathosformeln* (or, with a word he will introduce later: "dynamograms") are never the visual illustration of a concept or meaning. They are believed to *interrupt* spiritual stability and figural calm.[16]

Like Deligny, hence, Warburg believes in a kind of "memory of the species" that recovers an unsuspected vitality in long-forgotten

[15] Warburg, 'Dürer and Italian Antiquity', in *The Renewal of Pagan Antiquity*, 555. Cf. Sigrid Weigel's distinction between, on the one hand, the "*bewegtes Beiwerk*" and "excited gestures" (*erregte Gebärden*) that are mentioned in the Boticelli-essay and, on the other, the *Pathosformeln* pure and proper that are introduced in the essay on Dürer twelve years later. The former refer to the "memory of ancient gestures in Renaissance visual art and the associated epistemological shift of the gaze from *work* to *by-work* (*Beiwerk*)." The latter refer to the "revival of ancient drama traditions in courtly festivities." See Sigrid Weigel, "'Von Darwin über Filippino zu Botticelli ... und ... wieder zur Nymphe.' Zum Vorhaben einer energetischen Symboltheorie und zur Spur der Darwin-Lektüre in Warburgs Kulturwissenschaft," in *Warburgs Denkraum. Formen. Motive. Materialen*, ed. Martin Treml, Sabine Flach, Pablo Schneider (München: Wilhelm Fink, 2014), 146.

[16] See for instance Warburg's reference to the "emotive formulas" in Ghirlandaio's Tornabuoni frescoes which, "(o)nce freed ... could no longer be kept discreetly at a distance." In Warburg, "Francesco Sassetti's Last Injunctions to His Sons", 249. Gombrich notoriously presented the thesis that Warburg's interpretation of the *Pathosformel* shifted throughout the years. According to Gombrich, Warburg came to regard it as a "threat" and "negative influence" while it "stood originally for liberation from the restrictive bonds of realistic costume painting." In Ernst Gombrich, *Aby Warburg*, 177.

things and elements of nature.[17] Moreover, he, too, will put his finger on the human ability to break through the boundaries of the self at crucial moments. *Pathosformeln* are no expressions of a "lived experience" that strengthens the coherence of a self: they uproot the stability of the ego and thereby open up new ways of feeling, thinking, and acting. This awareness is the result of a trip to the United States, which took place more than 25 years prior to his arrival at Bellevue. When Warburg travels through the southern states in 1896 and stays with the Puebloans, he is fascinated by their snake rituals. The practices in which Indians take live snakes into their mouths are part of an intricate rain dance but, above all, they show that a de-self-ing can be accompanied by a regained sense of *agency*. Warburg argues that the snakes have a symbolic power, which stems from the fact that they are but "minimally visible to the eye" and should be considered "a usurping imposter" (*ein verdrängender Vergleicher*).[18] The efficacy of such symbols and symbolic practices cannot be explained with the jargon of phenomenology and existentialism: they do not prepare the work of stable perception and understanding that refashions the universe into a stable life-world. The snake, above all, incorporates those very features of the world that are bound to problematize the instrumentarium of human reason. It derails thought's ambition to synthesize the unformed material of the world into harmonious forms, remaining inseparable from nature's unending irregularities and transformations. In the words of Warburg, the serpent "experiences through

[17] See, among others, Aby Warburg, "Sandro Botticellis 'Geburt der Venus' und 'Frühling,'" "Dürer und die italienische Antike," "Ninfa Fiorentina," and "Florentinische Wirklichkeit und antikisirender Idealismus," in *Werke*, 39–123, 176–182, 198–210, and 211–233, respectively.

[18] Warburg, *Images from the Region of the Pueblo Indians*, transl. Michael Steinberg (Ithaca: Cornell University Press, 1995), 55. See also Papapetros' interesting analysis of these notes in Spyros Papapetros, "The Movement of Snakes. Pneumatic Impulses and Bygone Appendages from Philo to Warburg," in *On the Animation of the Inorganic. Art, Architecture, and the Extension of Life* (Chicago, London: The University of Chicago Press, 2012), 92.

the course of a year the full life cycle from deepest, deathlike sleep to the utmost vitality." It "changes its slough and (nonetheless) remains the same."[19] The serpent, and the symbol as such, is, literally, meta-morphosis: its being, or rather becoming, lies beyond all form.

Through interaction with these snakes, the Puebloans, too, undergo a profound metamorphosis: they "form(ed) themselves into a causal factor in order of things."[20] While there is of course no *real* impact on the weather, the intricate rituals and dances have a liberating effect nonetheless. The intense focus and careful execution of these symbolic practices neutralize the feeling of being merely passive. The Puebloans are now no longer just at the mercy of Mother Nature's whims: they are capable of truly interacting with her.

Like Deligny, Warburg regards this creative de-self-ing as proof that one's identity is only a provisional construction. Being-human is related to "the instability of the sense of self on account of the factuality of the bodily relation to an outside world of things."[21] He sets himself the challenge of understanding that this fluid boundary between man and thing is in fact the driving force of creativity. And here, as well, genuine creativity has to do with a thoroughly *corporeal* experience of the body and the possibility of becoming a *thing among things*. This means that Warburg, like Deligny, puts forward a theory of feeling-*out*, rather than feeling-in (em-pathy) or feeling-with (sym-pathy). In sharp opposition to Binswanger, who stipulates that genuine interaction is only possible on the basis of a shared "life" among human individuals, Warburg, like Deligny, underlines the importance of our capacity to "feel-out" to inorganic, *dead* things. For Warburg and Deligny, it is crucial to come to terms with forces that inevitably threaten the ego's internal stability. In the

---

[19] Warburg, *Images from the Region of the Pueblo Indians*, 55.

[20] Aby Warburg, "Bilder aus dem Gebiet der Pueblo-Indianer in North America," in *Werke*, 557.

[21] Aby Warburg, "Symbolismus als Umfangsbestimmung," in *Werke*, 619.

spring of 1896, while staying in New York, Warburg jots down a series of notes that is highly relevant in this regard. These would later underlie the "Reise-Erinnerungen aus dem Gebiet der Pueblo Indianer in Nordamerika" which were drafted during his stay in Binswanger's institution in 1923. These unpublished writings are indispensable to flesh out the opposition between Warburg's thoughts and those of Binswanger, and to pinpoint the affinities with Deligny. Like Binswanger, Warburg describes the inherent openness of the human being, yet, contrary to his therapist's view, he believes the psycho-physical nature of this openness to result in unavoidable mental lability: "the lability of the ego-feeling on account of the events that make up of the physical relation with the physical outside world" [*die Labilität des Ichgefühles durch die Thatsachen des körperlichen Verhaltens zur körperlichen Außerwelt*].[22] It is this physical interaction with the objects that surround us which, according to Warburg, inevitably results in limit-experiences that blur the line between life and death. Warburg builds on the idea that, as a "handling" [*hantierende*] being, man is fated to engage with dead objects that perpetually endanger his inner life and sense of self: "the borders of the person are fluctuating." This structural disequilibrium between man and world is nothing short of "tragic": "The starting point is the following; I consider man as an animal who handles things, whose activity consists in establishing connections and separations. This makes him lose his organic feeling of the self because indeed the hand allows him to seize concrete objects, which do not have a nervous apparatus because they are inorganic, but which nevertheless extend his self in an inorganic way. Here is the tragedy of the man who, by handling things, extends beyond his organic limit."[23]

With the notion of an unavoidable, tragic "incorporation" of dead objects, Warburg turns the fundamentals of Binswanger's

[22] Ibid., 619.
[23] Aby Warburg, "Reise-Erinnerungen aus dem Gebiet der Pueblo Indianer," in *Werke*, 580.

philosophy their head. For Binswanger, our inherent openness to the world prepares the path for a genuine *koinonia*: it is the condition for a shared space, in which we expand the region of the "lived" self and meaningfully interact with other individuals and objects. This entails that we, so to speak, breathe life into the "external" nature of the outside world: we learn to recognize other individuals as similar to us and gauge the ways in which objects can be meaningfully dealt with. In Warburg's account, to the contrary, our "empathic" abilities do not subjectify, vitalize, or "enliven" the external world: they do not modify the world into a "*life*-world" that is tuned to the moods of the self. To the contrary, this uncanny affinity with "something ... which corresponds to him, but which does not flow in his veins" pushes the human being beyond his limits altogether and installs the danger of a "loss of the subject in the object" [*Verlust des Subjekts an das Objekt*].

However, and most crucially, Warburg distinguishes three ways by which this mental threat and the ego's collapse *can be warded off.* They revolve around three different manners to interact with the physical world and are framed as the three types of "symbolization" that characterize human activity. For Warburg symbolization is in the first place an *Umfangsbestimmung*.[24] Warburg inherits this concept from Kant, in whose writings it stands for the determination of the "extension of a class." Kant uses the term *Umfangsbestimmung* to describe the logical formation of concepts, that is, to explain how conceptual thought identifies the shared qualities through which specific sensuous phenomena can be brought together within the same category. At times, Warburg's use of the term *Umfangsbestimmung* does point in that direction. For the mathematical-conceptual language of science is one of the three main instantiations of "symbolization as an *Umfangsbestimmung*." A mathematical-conceptual interaction with the outside world pertains to man's ambition to "understand" [*begreifen*]. Exemplified by

[24] All following quotes come from Warburg, "Symbolismus als Umfangsbestimmung," 615–628.

the human ability to speak and write, such an interaction with the physical world revolves around a "comparing" [*vergleichende*] approach that scans sensuous objects and phenomena for their resemblances. Man's ability to "understand" the world by way of mathematical-conceptual language thus installs a salutary "distance" [*Entfernung*] from his concrete surroundings and enables him to assert a sense of mastery over them. In those places of his oeuvre where Warburg is most optimistic about the progress of human reason, he presents the installment of such a happy interval vis-à-vis the world as the telos of historical and cultural evolution. There he presupposes a beneficial evolution away from embodied, pagan rituals, such as the serpent dances of the Puebloans, with the help of the conceptual instrumentarium of logical thought and linguistic syntax. When the Puebloans incorporate an external object by literally taking serpents in their mouth, for instance, this is not a merely irrational practice: in setting up a lived interaction between themselves and an external thing, they connect two radically different elements, not unlike the copula (e.g., the verb "is") which links up a subject with a predicate in a basic sentence. "The incorporation as a logical act of primitive culture [*die Verleibung als logischer Akt der primitiven Kultur*] … We have the simple sentence in statu nascendi where the subject and the object can amalgamate in case of loss of the copula, or destroy each other if the accent changes place. This state of an unstable rudimentary sentence composed of three elements is reflected in the religious artistic practice of the primitive people insofar as we can observe in their tendency to incorporate the object of a process parallel to that of the syntax."[25]

This mathematical-conceptual response to the world, geared to the ambition to "understand," is but one of three distinct types of symbolizations, and far from the most intriguing one. Warburg's analysis of symbolization as *Umfangsbestimmung* presupposes first

[25] Warburg, 'Reise-Erinnerungen,' 590, see also Christopher D. Johnson, *Memory, Metaphor, and Aby Warburg's Atlas of Images* (Ithaca, New York: Cornell University Press, 2012), 32–34.

of all that we can actively respond to a universe that is *not* attuned to our apparatus of understanding and stubbornly resists our search for meaning. In Warburg's account, what lies outside the ego is not a not-yet-formed world, waiting to be *formed* and *known*, but a radically form*less* universe that thwarts the logical calm of linguistic syntax and the categories of conceptual understanding. Therefore, Warburg's second type of symbolization revolves around the human being as an "adjusting" [*angleichende*] and "grasping" [*greifende*] organism, rather than a "comparing" [*vergleichende*] and "understanding" [*begreifende*] one. Warburg focuses here on interactions with the outside world that are geared toward a "restless appropriation" [*erfolglosen Aneignung*] of the object within the subject.[26] This means that the "grasping" human being is not interested in the specificities of, nor the resemblances between, the sensuous objects and phenomena themselves since his sole concern is the production of an extended self. "State of appropriation by incorporation. Parts of the object remain in the state of appertained foreign bodies, thus prolonging in the inorganic domain the feeling of identity of the self."[27] Unlike the response of an "understanding" human being, the "grasping" human being's interaction with the world results in a "sublation of distance" [*Aufhebung der Entfernung*] but this does not jeopardize the stability of their ego. What matters most to the "grasping" human being is their ability to transmute the external object into a "painless body-part" [*schmerzlose Körpertheil*]. In Warburg's view, "handling" and "carrying/wearing" [*tragen*] are the most foundational exemplifications of this second type of symbolization, with "possessing" and "active wearing" [*Schmuck, Gerät, Tracht*] being listed as successful ways to re-establish the central position of man in the universe.[28]

[26] Warburg, "Symbolismus als Umfangsbestimmung," 624.

[27] "The pursuing (handling) grasping man has had a temporary impression of an object in the distance, and in order to strengthen this fleeting (stimulus) he completes it arbitrarily in order to recreate or re-evoke (this) individual stimulus of the mobile, independently detached thing." In ibid., 625.

[28] Ibid., 617.

The third type of "symbolization as *Umfangsbestimmung*" is undoubtedly the most intriguing one, and the most relevant to set up an (im)possible dialogue with Binswanger and Deligny. Apart from man's "comparing" [*vergleichende*] and "adjusting" [*angleichende*] attitudes, Warburg mentions the possibility of a "compensating" [*ausgleichende*] response to the world. It is this third type of psycho-physical interaction with the world that he calls "creative" [*bildend*]. Like the attempt to "understand" or "grasp" the world, the "creative" attitude is capable of warding off the "loss of the subject in the object." However, the "creative" interaction with the world is the most complex of all three possible types of symbolization because a physical proximity to the world is here believed to go *hand in hand* with the creation of a mental distance from it. Earlier, we mentioned this precise paradox as the inspiration behind Deligny's project, where a direct interaction with objects and phenomena in the world is believed to open a creative line of flight *from* the world. In Warburg's jargon this same idea is expressed in the following manner: "*Through conscious subjective corporealization* [Verkörperung] *the distance is really destroyed but regained in the mind as consciousness, the consciousness of distance settles in the brain as memory.*"[29] In the multiple sketches that visualize his views of symbolization, Warburg places the "creative" interaction with the world in-between the "comparing," "describing," "understanding" "distance" from the world (science) and the "appropriating," "grasping" "sublation of distance" (immediate action).[30] In "creative" activity, it is precisely the human being's direct engagement with dead, material phenomena which installs an interval vis-à-vis the world. "The work of art is a product of the *repeated* attempt on the part of the subject to put a distance between himself and the object."[31] This paradox hinges on Warburg's reference to the "feeling-touching-scanning" [*abtastende*] attitude of the creative human

---

[29] Ibid., 622.
[30] Ibid., 626.
[31] Ibid., 618.

being. A creative responsiveness to the outside world is above all marked by an "oscillating attentiveness" and a careful interaction between "warding off and drawing near" [*abstossen and auslösen*]. In such a meticulous interaction with external objects, they can be simultaneously approached *and* kept at a distance, however puzzling this may sound: the creative response to the world hinges on an "intuitive touching/feeling/scanning without the will to appropriate" [*reflexmäßiges Abtasten ohne den Willen zur Annäherung*] and therefore results in a "distance within the near-at-hand" [*Entfernung in der Greifnähe*] and a "dynamic tension" [*dynamischer Spannungszustand*].[32] In the creative attitude, the retrieval of a liberating freedom is *inseparable from* and *compensates for* man's direct exposure to lifeless things. No doubt, the images of *Janmari* painstakingly handling a ball of clay with a string are a fine illustration of this restorative "oscillating attentiveness" and the precarious interplay between "warding off and drawing near."

Warburg radically questions the human being's central and controlling position in the world. He does not believe that "lived" experiences can assuage the potentially disturbing impact of an otherwise chaotic universe. When Warburg refers to "creative" activity as a third type of *Umfangsbestimmung*, that term ought to be translated as the "determination of a contour." The "feeling/touching/scanning" attitude of "creative" symbolization is to Warburg above all else an attempt to come to terms with "the tangible coarseness of life" [*die greifbare derbe Lebensfülle*] through intense sensations. Such sensuous stimuli do partake in the chaos of the empirical world but they have a profoundly enlivening effect. In creative activity, the chaos of the world is given a proper "delineation" and thereby, to return to a word from Warburg's diaries, acquires a "lucidity" of its own. This means that, in the creative experience of certain things and events, a seeming lack of order nonetheless fixates the observer's gaze and draws it nearer. This seeming sensuous disorder does not leave man passive or powerless since, within it, a unique logic is established that enables the perceiver or, indeed, the

---

[32] Ibid. 624–626.

youngsters in Deligny's network, to react, feel, and think for themselves. Like Deligny, Warburg explores how the chaos of the senses need not be tamed by the quest for a universal language or a shared world. The "logic" of such intense sensations is *sui generis* since they neither thrive on linguistic references nor on the ambition to fully rid the outside world of its uncontrollable features.

* * *

In addition to Warburg's unwavering belief in the therapeutic power of his own thinking and the similarities to Deligny's project there may be a second reason for the favorable course of his therapeutic process. The therapeutic account that Binswanger wrote about Warburg is already very different from his study of *Ellen*. Here there is no "humanly impossible" behavior or manifest *Todgeweihtheit*. On the contrary, Binswanger soon becomes fascinated by the "interesting transition from (Warburg's) scientific views to individual delusions" and seems to share his view that his research interests can be a saving grace.[33] This seems to be the starting point for a very different therapeutic approach. In contrast to *Ellen*, who is visited by Binswanger only twice per day and for very short sessions, Warburg is taken seriously as an intellectual from day one.[34] From Warburg's arrival in Bellevue onward, Binswanger attempts to rekindle his passion for art and science. In the first days of his stay, Warburg is still too far gone to appreciate such attempts. When Binswanger refers to a literary source in one of their first conversations, he is rebuffed by Warburg: "How can you dress up your treatment with cultural glitter [*Bildungsflitter*]?"[35] Later, then,

---

[33] Binswanger, quoted in *Die unendliche Heilung*, 21.

[34] For criticisms of Binswanger's therapeutic approach and overly "scientific" methodologies, see the work of Carl Rogers, primarily *On Becoming a Person* (London: Little, Brown Book Group, 1963) and R.D. Laing, primarily *The Voice of Experience: Experience, Science and Psychiatry* (New York: Penguin Books, 1983).

[35] From the medical report of April 19, 1921, in *Die unendliche Heilung*, 37.

Binswanger does manage to revive Warburg's scholarly interest and regularly invites him to his home for tea, where he shows him around his library. He offers him books, such as Hans Prinzhorn's *Bildnerei der Geisteskranken*. The emotional and intellectual bond developed between the two men is authentic and profound and will culminate in a correspondence that lasts for years. Moreover, Binswanger asks his patient to make public presentations about his research interests within the walls of the institution. Thus, on April 21, 1923, the famous "Lecture on the Snake Ritual" takes place in which Warburg shares his findings on the snake ritual of the Puebloans. His audience includes fellow patients, doctors, and nurses. Binswanger also invites prominent intellectuals to engage in conversation with Warburg to further his research project. Ernst Cassirer's visit on April 10, 1924, will be a therapeutic breakthrough. By the summer of 1924, his increased mental stability has become apparent to all.

It is tempting to attribute the positive outcome of Warburg's therapeutic process to Binswanger's approach. Does this not provide the best evidence that a humanistic, individual-centered *Daseinsanalyse works?* That possibility cannot be ruled out. Binswanger's plea to put the *human being* at the center of psychiatry deserves to be heard at all times. In the case of Warburg, Binswanger did succeed in restoring his "motivational structure" and "mental life." But even this awareness cannot fully cancel out the sentiment that Warburg's recovery might in an essential way have been due to the "human" reactive and creative capacity that both he and Deligny so meticulously put their finger on. For *Ellen's* fate, of course, the happy ending of Warburg's story makes no difference whatsoever. But if his story could count as an illustration of the power of "reacting" and "creating," it increases the impression that a "spider's web" of gestures and "points of reference" could have taken shape even within the walls of Bellevue. This would at least free up a small, imaginary space for the possibility that even *Ellen's* condition was never entirely beyond hope.

INDEX[1]

[1] Note: Page numbers followed by 'n' refer to notes.

77

GPSR Compliance

The European Union's (EU) General Product Safety Regulation (GPSR) is a set of rules that requires consumer products to be safe and our obligations to ensure this.

If you have any concerns about our products, you can contact us on ProductSafety@springernature.com

In case Publisher is established outside the EU, the EU authorized representative is:

Springer Nature Customer Service Center GmbH
Europaplatz 3
69115 Heidelberg, Germany

The manufacturer's authorised representative in the EU is Springer
Nature Customer Service Centre GmbH, Europaplatz 3, 69115 Heidelberg,
Germany. If you have any concerns regarding our products, please
contact ProductSafety@springernature.com

Printed and bound by CPI Group (UK) Ltd, Croydon, CR0 4YY

24/04/2026
02096315-0006